Heal Yourself

Heal Yourself:

Unlock **Your Healing Energies** and **Transform Your Life**

By **John Lake**

Contents

Introduction

"Sometimes it's not enough to just survive," I said with a frown.

The psychologist nodded, sympathetic.

"I know, John. That's why you're here."

"See, that's what I thought, but now I'm not so sure," I retorted.

I clenched my fists. I wanted to hit something, but what can you hit in a psychologist's office? The soft, luxurious couches? The pastel curtains? The solid mahogany desk? The fake ferns? Right, nothing. I gritted my teeth and clenched my fists instead.

"I thought I would find some answers here but I haven't found anything yet. You know what today is? It's a full year since I started coming here, and nothing, so far. Nothing!"

"I'm sorry you feel that way," said my psychologist.

He was being honest. He really did feel bad. That didn't make me feel better, but it did make me feel a bit ashamed for lashing out.

"I'm just so lost," I said. "Where am I going? What am I doing with my life?" I picked at the couch where some of the fabric was coming undone.

At this point, I was in my late twenties, with enough hair left that I could still call it a "full head of hair," growing a bit pudgy around the waist but not exactly in bad shape. But I was in dire straits, emotionally. I had a dead end job, I had recently been dumped. I was in a strange city with very few friends, and I was not, in any way, "living the dream." Unless, of course, the dream is to be miserable.

I felt like there was something missing. I knew *why* I was depressed, and I still couldn't fix the problem. I knew *why* I was putting on weight, but I couldn't get the motivation to exercise. I knew *why* I didn't have many friends left, but I found it impossible to meet new people. When I did meet people, I inevitably scared them off with a combination of neediness and control issues.

So what's a poor, confused young adult to do? I went to therapy, a full year of therapy with no luck. That's how we got to this scene.

Take The FREE 3-Minute Chakra Healing Test. Find out how each of your 7 Chakras may be influencing your health and life

www.VelocityHousePresents.com/chakrahealing

1

This book is for anyone who's ever felt like they were living life the wrong way. Maybe it's because of depression and feeling lost, as it once was for me. Maybe you feel like you put too much faith in money, or that you give away too much power to others. Perhaps you harbor grudges too long, finding it hard to forgive even minor grievances. Maybe you just feel vulnerable, or you're afraid of public speaking, or you're constantly sexually frustrated. Maybe your relationships never work out, and you've lost every friend you held dear, because you didn't know how to act.

Whatever your specific ailment, it doesn't have to be that way. There's a way to get your life back on track. It's easy, it's inexpensive, and it will completely change your quality of life. If you've ever dreamed of living a fulfilled and happy life, but have never quite figured out how to do so, you've picked up the right book. I've spent years honing my craft prior to writing this book.

Why? Because I was you, at one point. I used to spend my days aimlessly, desperately wishing for guidance. I couldn't figure out what to do or where to turn to. I felt like the world had failed me, like I had fallen between the proverbial cracks and into some nether-realm. I drank too much and ate too little (although it was all junk). And I sabotaged anything that even came close to being termed a "relationship."

Yet, I learned how to get myself out of that rut, and you can, too. More than that, this book is going to awaken you to a whole new philosophy. I'm not giving you an instant fix. Instead, this book will revolutionize the way you live, teaching you to keep both your mind and body healthy, provided you're ready to accept this knowledge. You're going to learn to approach the world in an entirely different way.

I stopped picking at the couch, vaguely aware that my psychologist was speaking to me.

"Same time next week?" he said, desperately clinging to some semblance of optimism, even in the face of my anger and frustration.

God bless the man, he really tried to do his job. It's just too bad that I couldn't use the help he offered. I needed something else. I needed something better.

"Sure," I said, and walked out.

It was a lie. I never went back to visit that psychologist. Later that same week, I found a different philosophy.

Take The FREE 3-Minute Chakra Healing Test. Find out how each of your 7 Chakras may be influencing your health and life

2

www.VelocityHousePresents.com/chakrahealing

CHAPTER 1

A New You

I find it a bit poignant to begin this book on New Year's Eve, a day where many will promise to better themselves in the coming year. My goal is to help you achieve that purpose. I want to help you discover "the new you," just as I discovered "the new me."

It was fifteen years ago that I started down this path. I was a wounded young man. I was vulnerable, angry, and very sad. It's hard to put my finger on what initially caused my dark feelings. The triggering events were ongoing, vicious and repetitive occurrences, making it hard to designate one as the "first." I was in a rocky relationship which was falling apart. Following close behind, was the death of a person close to me. Add to that a frustration with my (lack of) career, and a general all-purpose malaise in my life. All of the subconscious destructiveness in my life began to overflow.

I was a confused and lost twenty-something with too little time, too little money, and too much resentment. I began looking for something to help me. The truth is, I couldn't find much. If I'd lived in the 1950s, they would have given me a Valium prescription to blunt all my emotions at once. Thankfully my experience in the 1990's was better than that, however it did not provide the relief I was hoping for.

I went to a psychologist, with visions of soft couches and probing questions in my head. My psychologist was a nice guy, thin and fighting

Take The FREE 3-Minute Chakra Healing Test. Find out how each of your 7 Chakras may be influencing your health and life

www.VelocityHousePresents.com/chakrahealing

3

a losing battle against gray hair. There was a lot of leather and impressive-looking books in his office, with very few traces of modernism, actually, which I liked at the time. He looked respectable, intelligent and sympathetic.

Unfortunately, while he was all of these things and more, he didn't have the answers I needed. I tried. I really did. I went and talked with him for a year, each time hoping that this would be the day of the "breakthrough," or (in other words), the day when I could finally stop driving half an hour out of my way to go to therapy.

That day never came.

It wasn't his fault. I began to understand more about myself, at least. We uncovered a lot of events in my past that were at the root of my current issues, and I got to peek at the mental gears and mechanisms that made John Lake (me) do what he did on a daily basis.

If you've ever suffered from pervasive depression, however, you know that it's not quite enough to *understand* your depression. I felt stuck. I felt paralyzed by events I only half-remembered from distant days in my past. I felt like everyone around me had these great things happening, while I just sat there getting older.

After a year of therapy, with very little improvement, I began looking for something else to help. I was a frustrated, depressed, angry, slightly older twenty-something, and still confused about where I was going in life. I felt disconnected from everything and everyone. I was angry at God and skeptical about my spirituality.

Now, I was never very spiritual, even at the best of times. I didn't even care if there was some God watching over me. If there was, I thought he or she was a jerk for letting all this happen to me. I didn't feel anything deep in my life. I believed in what was in front of me and nothing else.

So when my neighbor first mentioned the ancient philosophy Reiki to me, I balked. Manipulating my body's energies? Reconnecting to my chakras? What is this, and what does it even mean?

I turned away from it. I purposefully cut myself off from a potential healing technique, solely because it seemed too weird, too ancient, and too spiritual for a barely-believing young male. My "rational" brain rejected it. I couldn't understand Reiki, and I couldn't take it. It was, for lack of a better term, weird!

Take The FREE 3-Minute Chakra Healing Test. Find out how each of your 7 Chakras may be influencing your health and life

4   *www.VelocityHousePresents.com/chakrahealing*

Lucky for me, I was desperate. After months of declining my neighbor's Reiki advances, I swallowed my pride and gave in. She set me up with a friend, and off I went to study. "John, what have you got yourself into?" I wondered as I drove to my first session.

Within three years, I was the guy *teaching* people about Reiki. I was a bit older, but this time well-adjusted, purposeful, and *happy*, with a lot to offer the world. This was all because I listened to my neighbor. I thank her every day for lifting me out of that rut and giving me the advice I needed, even though she knew I would be skeptical of her initial advances.

I tell you this story because I know it can be intimidating when you first approach "Eastern mysticism," on the long road to healing yourself. First you have to force yourself to look past the Western medical tradition. If you're like me, this step could be the hardest. Most of us are only introduced to Western medicine from an early age. This makes it hard to know where else to turn when what we know and rely on fails us. I stayed with my psychologist for far too long, simply because I didn't know there were alternatives.

Next, you have to accept those alternatives. You have to be willing to give these "strange" techniques a try. I went into my first Reiki session very confused, and convinced that I'd betrayed my rational self by looking into these other treatment options.

My reaction was entirely unfounded. I hope you don't make the same mistakes. I hope you've sought out this book much earlier in the process, so you can work out whatever it is that troubles you before wasting more time on ineffective methods.

Whether you're a newcomer seeking help, or a long-time devotee to the understanding of the chakras, I hope you'll find this book refreshing and helpful.

A little background for the newcomers: the chakras are "a series of wheel-like vortices which exist in the surface of the etheric double of man."[i] In other words, they are wells of vital life energy residing in your body. The chakras are intertwined with major parts of your body (such as your feet and your groin), helping to keep you physically healthy. Each also relates to some aspect of your spiritual and emotional health. Properly maintained chakras will keep your life running smoothly, from your sex life, to your self-esteem, and your willingness to commit to relationships.

Need an analogy? Compare these to your body's nervous or circulatory systems, except that your chakras carry your life force instead of electrical signals or blood. The chakra "system" interacts with the other systems in your body, and it must also be maintained.

The chakras are changing. It might sound strange for such an ancient concept, but the truth is that these are not immobile or inflexible ideas. Some of the changes arise because of our own breakthroughs—we understand the chakras better the more we study them. Other changes, however, occur in the very nature of the chakras. They adapt and evolve to our own fluctuating lifestyles. The 90s, when I first studied Reiki, were very different than today.

The chakras are changing with the times, as they've done in the past. The purpose for each chakra is continually adapting to the changes around us. People are having new experiences, new breakthroughs, in relation to the metamorphosis of the chakras. We finally understand why our old knowledge of these chakras isn't quite in line with what's happening to people *right* now, and we can move to address those discrepancies.

If you're new to studying the chakras, congratulations. You've picked the right book, because now you're on the forefront of this next wave of information. By reading this, you're getting the most up-to-date depiction of the chakras.

If you're a long-time adherent, however, you'll get just as much out of this book. You'll probably be amazed how much has changed since the last time you sat down and really studied the chakras. I know I was amazed, when comparing my initial encounter to the chakra system in the 90's, to our present-day knowledge. There's indeed been a large shift, and knowing what's going on with these new energies will help you immensely. Being sensitive of these changes will make you more efficient and more prepared for the future. I think you'll be amazed.

I'm ready to help you clear out all of your old training, or, if you're a newcomer, to get you past the unfamiliarity surrounding the philosophy of the chakras. Let me guide you through these changes and teach you how to make use of them. I'm ready to help you overcome the

Take The FREE 3-Minute Chakra Healing Test. Find out how each of your 7 Chakras may be influencing your health and life

6   www.VelocityHousePresents.com/chakrahealing

obstacles that you confront every day, and to help you lead a healthier, more productive life.

I ask is that you keep an open mind. You're going to learn a lot in this book, no matter how much background knowledge you have. It will require effort on your part to take in and apply what you learn. You may be confused at first or hit a plateau. Just keep trying. Really immerse yourself in this philosophy, and I promise you'll be amazed at how your life changes. Discover a "new you." In fifteen years, maybe it will be you writing a book on the development of the chakras.

The chakras are present whether or not you acknowledge them. I turned away from the chakras when I first encountered them, believing that my neighbor, while kindhearted, was ultimately misled about my afflictions. That didn't mean the chakras disappeared. All it meant was that my problems persisted. Ignoring the chakras doesn't solve the issue; it just prolongs the suffering.

You really will discover a completely new way of looking at your problems. Once you learn how to influence your life by manipulating your chakra energies, you won't ever go back. You'll be amazed that you spent eighteen or twenty-five or fifty or a hundred years trying to solve your problems the old way. The chakras will seem natural. All you have to do is read and put the information into practice.

As for how to read this book and learn the information, methods may vary. Of course, there's always the traditional "start-to-finish" method, and that's definitely effective. If you're a beginner, this might be a good starting point. You'll get all the information, both new and old. We'll work from the lowest chakras—the foundations—up to the higher ones, so this approach will also make sense as we move from section to section. Read a chapter before every session, in the order they're presented in the book, and allow each chapter to build upon the ones that came before.

I recommend you work twice a week for an hour, meditating on your chakras using the exercises I present to you. One chapter per session, twice a week, assists your body in making essential changes without getting overwhelmed. You could do more, you could do less—everyone's different. Try changing the frequency or length of your sessions, however, if you experience any issues with the program. You might be over- or under-working your chakras.

Once you've finished the entire book, you'll recognize that you need to give additional attention to certain areas or chakras. At that point, your reading approach might change. If you've already read the book once, or if you're a veteran to these ideas, feel free to find the chapter that concerns you. Are you experiencing problems with your sacral or crown chakra? You can always turn straight to those sections and start reading. Don't force yourself to read through the chapters you don't need if you're looking for immediate help, and you already know what you're doing. Just use the information you need to get things back on track.

You could also try out this more spontaneous approach right from the start, even as a newcomer to the subject. However, you may feel a bit more confused than if you approached the book in a linear manner. Still, you must decide which is the most efficient learning method for you.

Let's start right away with the new chakra information. The first chapter will cover the "foot chakra" or "chakra zero," which we're only recently beginning to understand. For beginners, this is a great starting place, because it's the base that all of our other chakras are built upon. Even if you've practiced these philosophies before, my method will teach you quite a bit of new information right away.

It's time to reveal the new you.

Take The FREE 3-Minute Chakra Healing Test. Find out how each of your 7 Chakras may be influencing your health and life

8   *www.VelocityHousePresents.com/chakrahealing*

CHAPTER 2

Chakra Zero:
The Foot Chakra

"I feel lost."

He sounded it, too. In fact, I'd never heard my friend Dave sound so vulnerable. "I thought I knew where I was heading in life," he said, "but now...with everything that's happened..."

Dave had been through a rough couple of months. He'd been fired from his job, and he didn't really know what to do next. His inability to act was causing problems in his relationship. He felt keenly aware that his wife was drifting away from him, her sympathy turning to resentment. Worse, he didn't know how to fix the situation.

"Look down at your feet," I told him.

Our "foot chakra" or "chakra zero" is what connects us to Earth.[ii] When we aren't properly tuned in to our foot chakra, we feel lost or disconnected. We feel discouraged. We feel unsure about the future. The foot chakra is what gives us purpose, keeps us moving forward and shows us the path through life.

The "foot chakra" is not actually an entirely separate chakra, even though I will treat it as such. It's one half of your root chakra, which is the subject of the next chapter. We might call it the "bottom half" of the

Take The FREE 3-Minute Chakra Healing Test. Find out how each of your 7 Chakras may be influencing your health and life
www.VelocityHousePresents.com/chakrahealing

9

root chakra. However, it's easier referring to it as the foot chakra, and this is how many practitioners refer to this area as well.

The foot chakra, true to its name, is located on the bottom of your feet, however it encompasses more than that. While it inhabits the balls of your feet, it's simultaneously mixed with part of the Earth itself. The energy flowing out of your feet and into the ground fuses the two together.

Think of the foot chakra as a giant plate you're standing on. It's a big magnet that follows you around as you move, keeping you grounded. It keeps you plugged in to the Earth's energy. It's your piece of Earth. It's your energy base.

Stretch your arm out as far as it can go and use your index finger to draw an imaginary circle on the ground. That is the space your foot chakra covers. Don't take this too literally—your foot chakra isn't just the little patch of carpet you just circled. It's the energy field that exists within the circle. That energy field moves with you wherever you go, and it's where we draw our purpose from.

If you've ever tried using the Law of Attraction, but without an awareness of the needs of your foot chakra, then you've been doing yourself a disservice. The Law of Attraction is the principle that "like attracts like."[iii] In other words, if you focus on positivity, further positive things will happen in your life. On the other hand, focusing on negativity can only attract more negativity.

Many people try practicing the Law of Attraction but get frustrated when they don't see results. They focus all of their energy on positivity but do not experience the change they desire. They're making one simple mistake. They're neglecting to give the Law of Attraction any grounding in reality. Thinking positive thoughts is a good practice, but we don't live in a thought-world. We don't live in our minds. Moving those positive thoughts into the physical realm is essential in order to experience the effect of those thoughts. We need to move the idea of abundance from our minds into the world around us.[iv]

The foot chakra provides the grounding necessary to accomplish this. It's the place where we manifest positive thoughts into reality. The foot chakra is the magnet that helps the Law of Attraction function.

When we disconnect from our foot chakra, we also disconnect from the Law of Attraction. We disconnect from the world. We feel lost and

Take The FREE 3-Minute Chakra Healing Test. Find out how each of your 7 Chakras may be influencing your health and life

10   www.VelocityHousePresents.com/chakrahealing

we feel vulnerable, because we can't draw positivity into our lives. We feel aimless. We can't figure out where to turn, because nothing is welcoming. Nothing is safe. Life feels chaotic.

Then we ground ourselves; we reconnect to our foot chakra, and everything makes sense again. We can clearly see our path laid out before us. We feel purposeful again. We feel our foot chakra attracting positivity into our lives. We can see what needs to occur, and we can see the steps necessary to get there. It's a relief, really.

I hesitate using the term "guardian angel," because that has so many connotations for people. Yet, the foot chakra essentially fills the role of a guardian angel. It watches out for you. It carries you through the hard times in life by providing you a clear, accessible path to the other side. It shows you where to go, regardless of how difficult life seems.

This is what I meant when I told Dave, "Look down at your feet." I wasn't ignoring his problems. I was quite literally giving him the advice that I felt could help him get out of his rut.

Dave said it himself: "I feel lost." It's the classic declaration of someone who isn't grounded, someone who isn't attuned to his or her foot chakra. Since I first met Dave, I'd known him to always be a man of purpose. Have you ever seen the film *It's a Wonderful Life?*[v] At one point, Jimmy Stewart's character says, "I know what I'm going to do tomorrow, and the next day, and the next year, and the year after that!" Dave was a lot like George Bailey.

That is, until everything in Dave's life fell apart. Then he had no idea where to turn and no idea what to do next. He was suddenly unsure of every move he made. When I told Dave to look at his feet, I was entirely serious. Our eyes are excellent at directing energy. We tend to focus our efforts on whatever we're looking at. When I told Dave to look at his feet, it was so he'd start directing energy at his foot chakra. I wanted him to really concentrate on his feet so that they would show him the way.

It worked! It took him a little while to get used to the idea. He's always respected what I do, but he's never been a huge participant. I saw the desperation in him, though. I saw his desire to change. He started going on long walks every day, just staring at his feet. He told me once that he'd leave his house looking down at his feet and get back home still

Take The FREE 3-Minute Chakra Healing Test. Find out how each of your 7 Chakras may be influencing your health and life

www.VelocityHousePresents.com/chakrahealing   **11**

looking at his feet, all without looking up once. He really took the advice to heart, and within a short while, he did get better. I'm sure he was sick of looking at his beat up shoes, but he started to see his life change.

Within a couple of weeks he had a plan of action. Within a month he'd found a new job, with higher pay and better benefits. Within a few more weeks, he'd gotten his relationship back on track, once again connecting with his wife. He was back to his old Jimmy Stewart ways. I'd never seen someone so motivated, except for the old Dave. It was an incredible change, which he accomplished in a short amount of time. Dave focused on his area of weakness, his foot chakra, and he transformed his issues and grounded his energy. Once he'd done that, and he started seeing a plan and the rest was easy.

I urge you to do the same if you feel lost or disconnected. Take a moment to assess your foot chakra. We're eventually going to asses our connection to each of the chakras in order to find your weaknesses. So let us begin.

Focus on your foot chakra. Feel the energy field down below you, keeping you grounded and "plugged in" to the Earth. Really immerse yourself in that connection. Now, on a one-to-ten scale, how connected do you feel to your foot chakra? How active is that connection? One means you feel no connection at all. If so, you are likely lost and confused, just like my friend Dave. Ten means the connection is strong and wide open. You are completely grounded, and you can feel the Law of Attraction at work. We'd love our connection to every chakra to be a ten, but that's difficult (if not impossible). If you're a newcomer to this philosophy, it's likely that your connection is nowhere near ten. Maybe it's even below five. That's fine! We're going to work on it.

Sometimes the answer is more complex than a number scale will allow. Maybe you find yourself very grounded, but you can't seem to manifest abundance in your life. In that case, maybe you create two separate ratings for those ideas. The number values are used just for us to assess weaknesses. Whatever you need to do to identify your own weaknesses, do so. I use one-to-ten ratings, because they are easily quantified.

You can certainly use other ways to assess your connection with your foot chakra: how do your feet feel at the end of the day; how organized do you feel, and how easy is it for you to focus on your goals?

Take The FREE 3-Minute Chakra Healing Test. Find out how each of your 7 Chakras may be influencing your health and life

12   www.VelocityHousePresents.com/chakrahealing

Once you are conscious of your current connection to your foot chakra, we can begin working on any deficiencies. The first step, as I said to Dave, is simply to look at your feet. Walk around town, or walk around the house. Look at your feet and focus your energy on them. This is literally the easiest technique you'll ever encounter. It takes no special time commitment and no special equipment, and minimal effort is required. Just look down, focus on your feet as you walk, and you'll automatically direct energy towards your foot chakra. It's so simple, but powerful. You will begin to feel more grounded.

To help aid the flow of energy, try creating a visual image for yourself. Picture the energy as it flows to your feet; what does it look like, what color is it?. Imagine how your feet would look when receiving that energy. It's like a warm beam of light shining out of your eyes and falling on your glowing feet. Use this visualization while walking to stimulate your awareness of your foot chakra.

Another technique I use, which also requires some visualization, is returning to the circle you drew on the ground. Remember when I asked you to stretch out your arm and trace a circle on the ground around you? Picture that circle again now.

Once you can clearly see the outline of your own foot chakra, push it outwards. Expand the boundary. Let it grow and encompass more of the ground you stand on. Imagine that this entire area fills with energy, like red-hot lava or beams of light rising up from the Earth. Focus on drawing that energy into your body. Picture it swirling towards you, entering your body through your feet. Before long, you should feel warmth in your feet, and a growing sense of purpose. The connection to your foot chakra is growing stronger. You should see your path laid out in front of you. And try to picture a glowing cord, starting at your feet and stretching far into the distance, keeping your life on course.

Whether you have worked with the chakras previous to reading this book or you are new to this philosophy, I imagine that you now understand the importance of the foot chakra. It is what grounds us, and connects us to purposeful living. Thus a blockage of the foot chakra will affect every other chakra. We need the foot chakra functioning correctly in order to draw in the energy used by the other chakras. We need that sense of purpose and fulfillment in order to keep the rest of our body

Take The FREE 3-Minute Chakra Healing Test. Find out how each of your 7 Chakras may be influencing your health and life

www.VelocityHousePresents.com/chakrahealing   **13**

functioning in a healthy state. There's a reason the foot chakra is below even the root chakra—it's our true foundation.

The greatest danger to the foot chakra comes when we pile on new experiences and new problems. It is difficult to feel grounded if you are constantly dealing with unfamiliar challenges. When we gradually introduce our foot chakra to changes, we help it build up strength. It's like exercise. You don't just wake up one day and run a marathon. You must train diligently in order for your body to endure 26.2 miles. You begin with shorter runs, and gradually they get longer and longer as the weeks progress. Eventually you're ready to run a full marathon.

The foot chakra works in a similar way. You must consistently work at keeping grounded while introducing your foot chakra to small changes and challenges. Once you feel solid in the day to day grounding of your foot chakra, you will be ready when the larger changes occur. New experiences and changes in your life will not throw off your balance, as it may have in the past. Your foot chakra, which is now firmly grounded, will naturally adapt to your changed circumstances.

If you are not prepared, and have not experienced the firm grounding of your energy through your foot chakra, disturbing changes can cause chaos in your life. When you are thrown into a turbulent situation, or an unfamiliar setting without the strength that comes from a well grounded foot chakra, you will be overwhelmed, and your energies become scattered.

If you are not practiced in keeping your foot chakra grounded, and have not worked bit by bit to test the strength of that grounding with small changes, the large events will throw you off, and your foot chakra may become blocked. This inhibits the flow of positive energy into your body. Once blocked, your situation can only grow worse. You'll feel aimless and lost, which will reinforce the negative feelings—and thereby reinforce the blockage. You need to focus on the foot chakra in order for energy to begin moving again, so that you can become grounded by the connected flow of energy between your foot chakra and the Earth.

Take a moment to go into this strange, uncomfortable energy. Picture the energy field in your mind. It's a chaotic mass of light and darkness, fighting for control. There will be a lot of swirling energies, a

Take The FREE 3-Minute Chakra Healing Test. Find out how each of your 7 Chakras may be influencing your health and life

14   www.VelocityHousePresents.com/chakrahealing

lot of disruptions, and none of the safety and security that we usually hope for in our energy reserves. This energy will feel foreign and make you feel uneasy, but you must immerse yourself in it before things can get better. Think of your best friend. At one point, your best friend was just a stranger. This energy field is the same way. Get in there and confront it, meet it, and turn it to your own purposes.

One mistake I witness all too often is the use of mental overlays. We love mental overlays, because they make us feel safe and secure. What do I mean? False positivity; putting spin on something; failing to confront the root of the issue, because you convince yourself it's not that bad. You lie to yourself.

The human brain hates failure. It doesn't like thinking about those possibilities. Thus, we have a tendency of downplaying the possibility of failure when we move into a new, uncomfortable experience. We'll say things like, "I'll be fine," or "I can do this," but we'll ignore that there's a problem. We ignore that our foot chakra is hurting. What we should be saying is, "I need to figure this problem out, or I will fail," or, "If I can't fix this problem, I will lose everything." Otherwise, we're simply putting a bandage over the wound instead of taking action.

Now, some of you might think, "But what about the Law of Attraction?" I've told you that thinking positive thoughts attracts more positivity, and this is true. The problem is that these mental overlays are not positive thoughts. They are merely deceptions. We don't actually believe them; they are simply a convenient method of ignoring the real problem. The problem's not going away. The false positivity is just a bandage—one that will rip off at the most inconvenient time possible, making everything worse in the process.

Don't let yourself use these overlays when you're connecting to your foot chakra. Embrace that uncomfortable energy. Embrace the idea of failure. Don't let it scare you. If you do it correctly, you'll feel it wrap around you. You'll feel that failure. It will make you sick. If you're truly connected to your foot chakra, you might even feel the soles of your feet tingling.

Get rid of that energy. Clear that sickening, failure-prone energy right out of the space. Use your feet and physically take over the space. A technique I employ with my clients involves kicking your feet out, ejecting the negative energy from the soles of your feet. You don't have to be a karate master. Just kick your feet firmly outwards, flinging the energy out of your space. Claim the space as your own.

If you want, feel free to state some affirmations out loud: "I'm releasing the fear that I'm going to lose everything," or, "I'm releasing my fear of failure." An affirmation is a positive statement that applies specifically to your situation, helping you heal.[vi] It is a supporting principle of the Law of Attraction, in that affirmations help us bring success and abundance into our lives. Repetition of affirmations gives them a hold in our thought processes and realigns the mental patterns of the brain.

Hopefully at this point, it's gone. All that negative energy, gone. It's not that we covered it up with positivity. It's that we embraced the problem and then kicked it out. It's not coming back. It will not flare up at an inconvenient moment. It's just not a factor anymore. You've cleared the blockage in your foot chakra, and you're ready for your new space.

Keep in mind that this process is not instantaneous for everyone. Most people will need successive sessions before they completely clear the blocks from their foot chakra. This is a process. Your work with the chakras is introducing an entirely new life philosophy to your body, not an instant cure. Reconnecting your chakras will take a little work on your part.

I recommend following this kicking exercise with the one that I mentioned earlier, where you picture your foot chakra as a circle on the ground and then try expanding the space outwards. Try pushing the boundaries of your foot chakra until it encompasses the entire space you've taken over. Say more affirmations, if you feel comfortable: "I am ready to use this new space," or, "I can see my path stretching before me."

Feel the energy entering you from your foot chakra and traveling throughout your body. It's there now. You're connected. You're ready to meet whatever challenges lie ahead, and you know what your plan is. You're Jimmy Stewart. You know what life holds, and you know that you can manage whatever surprises lie ahead. You don't fear failure. You can get through this. You're connected. You're grounded. You are ready to move forward. You are ready to manifest abundance in your life.

Take The FREE 3-Minute Chakra Healing Test. Find out how each of your 7 Chakras may be influencing your health and life

16   www.VelocityHousePresents.com/chakrahealing

CHAPTER 3

Chakra One:
The Root Chakra

At its core, the root chakra is about our human necessities. This includes three necessities in particular: money, health and relationships. An improperly balanced root chakra will cause strife in one or all of these areas of your life.

Once again, I'm going to give you the new information up front. I said that the root chakra deals with necessities, and that's still true. However, our understanding of this chakra has changed in the past few years to keep up with our ever-changing, ever-faster lifestyles.

We used to discuss the root chakra in terms of survival. If someone had enough money to survive, their root chakra must be fine. If they seemed fairly healthy and were surviving, they were fine. If their relationships weren't great, but they were surviving, that was perfect. As long as you were getting by, in other words, your root chakra didn't need any special attention. Survival was enough for the tribe as a whole, and that was all that mattered.

Get rid of that old idea. You and I both know that surviving is not enough. Just surviving is great, if there's no alternative, but there's more. If we were simply focused on survival, nothing would get done. We'd

Take The FREE 3-Minute Chakra Healing Test. Find out how each of your 7 Chakras may be influencing your health and life

www.VelocityHousePresents.com/chakrahealing   **17**

have no drive to invent or put in that extra hour of work on a project or take up a hobby. We'd be "surviving," but that's no way to live.

The terminology has changed. We now consider a healthy root chakra in terms of thriving. How are you doing with money? Are you thriving? Is your body really doing great? Are your relationships happy and stable? This is the way we live in the modern world. By thriving individually, we help the entire community. For too long, we were dealing with neglected root chakras without really noticing, because we thought survival was enough. Well, we can do better than simply surviving.

I'm sure you can already draw connections between the root chakra and the foot chakra. Feeling connected and satisfied with your future plans requires your foot chakra to be balanced, and the root chakra extends many of these same principles into more specific aspects of your well-being. This is why we call the foot chakra the "lower half" of the root chakra—they work in tandem.

There are specific traits that we associate with each chakra. Each chakra has a color, each chakra has an element, each chakra has a metal, and each chakra has an animal with which it's traditionally connected.[vii] These traits embody the energy we find in each chakra. For instance, the animal totem we join with each chakra symbolically relates to the principles of that chakra.[viii]

The root chakra, traditionally, is associated with the color red, the element earth, the metal lead and the snake animal totem.[ix] However, our new approach to the chakras is very concerned with individuality. It's about providing you with the best experience, bringing you more in touch with your personal needs. If you've worked with your chakras in the past, you may have different colors, elements or animals connected to your chakras, and that's fine. Bring those experiences with you to this book.

Focus on your root chakra now. If you're a beginner, delve into your root chakra. Picture a red-hot ball of energy around your groin and tailbone. It will be like molten lead, cradled in your hips. Probe that energy with your mind. Hold your hand over this area of your body, and feel the warmth radiating from your chakra. Hopefully you'll feel a strong connection to this energy reservoir, but if you don't, it's likely that your root chakra is unbalanced.

Take The FREE 3-Minute Chakra Healing Test. Find out how each of your 7 Chakras may be influencing your health and life

18   www.VelocityHousePresents.com/chakrahealing

So how does an unbalanced root chakra manifest itself? It depends, since you might have problems in one or more areas simultaneously. Let's split them out and go over them one at a time. As with your foot chakra, I recommend rating how closed off from each individual category you feel. For instance, someone who has problems with money may rate their root chakra's openness at zero. Someone who handles money with ease or feels confident drawing power from money, will rate their circumstance a ten in that category. Simultaneously, that person may struggle with their weight, so they'd rate their health aspect accordingly. If you are having issues in only one of the three categories (money, health, and relationships) you're welcome to skip ahead to the section that concerns you.

MONEY

If your root chakra is closed off and presenting issues in your fiscal life, you'll definitely know it. You'll frequently be in debt, or you may be impoverished. You're tired of being broke, but you can't really figure out how to fix that situation. Of course, this is often tied to an unbalanced foot chakra, because it also can signify a failure in attracting abundance into your physical realm.

When your root chakra is open, you'll handle money with confidence. You'll have money left over to do what you wish. You'll feel accomplished in your career and you will earn money with ease. Try carrying money around in your pocket every day—not just a credit or a debit card, but real cash. Feel the energy that money has. There's a reason they say money will "burn a hole in your pocket." There's a real energy you feel when you have cash money on hand. You can feel the money's presence. Bring some cash with you the next time you go out, and see if you feel more connected to your root chakra at the end of the day.

HEALTH

Each of the seven main chakras we'll talk about in this book are closely related to part of your physical body.[x] At the root chakra level, we're specifically discussing issues with your weight and immune system. Again, this is connected to the idea of the root chakra as something built on necessity. Problems with your weight or your general immune

Take The FREE 3-Minute Chakra Healing Test. Find out how each of your 7 Chakras may be influencing your health and life

www.VelocityHousePresents.com/chakrahealing

19

system are very easy to spot, and they're often the first things we notice when it comes to "bad health."

If you have a constant cold or a chronic cough, that may be your root chakra trying to get your attention. It wants your attention, so you will manipulate your life energies back into their healthy and balanced form. The same goes for weight issues. I'll assume you've tried losing weight at some point in your life. Almost everyone does. Are you obsessed with what the scale is telling you, though?

I've done it. I've battled the scale, weighing myself every night and hoping the number on the scale would drop a bit more. Paradoxically, I think the constant obsession with weight is hurting your cause. Your body knows how to be healthy. When you are constantly weighing yourself, you're bringing negative energy into your body. You're throwing off your body's natural rhythm and trying to force it into a new shape. You're not persuading your body—you're punishing your body. Stop! Let your body work it out. Accept your body. Give it permission to change, but don't force it into any particular shape. Open your root chakra, and let the energy enter your body of its own accord.

RELATIONSHIPS

If you're suffering from a neglected root chakra, you're going to feel like you don't belong or like you have to be somebody else to please your friends and family. I used to have this problem often when I went home. My parents still live in the same small town that I grew up in, and when I visited I'd find those old patterns still waiting for me. I'd interact with everyone—my parents, my old friends, the ancient manager of the town's only grocery store—as if I'd never left.

Even after I hadn't lived in that town for seven years, I would go home and act the same as I did when I graduated high school. That wasn't me. I wasn't a high school senior anymore. I wasn't even a college senior anymore. I had done seven years of growing up, of gaining experience and bringing these new life experiences to the table. When I went home, however, nobody wanted to see that side of me.

At least that's what I thought. It was ridiculous, of course. You have history with certain people, however, if they can't accept your new self,

Take The FREE 3-Minute Chakra Healing Test. Find out how each of your 7 Chakras may be influencing your health and life

20   www.VelocityHousePresents.com/chakrahealing

don't force yourself into old patterns of behavior. Those old patterns are hurtful. Those old patterns stifle your root chakra. Those old patterns deserve to be broken.

Sure, you could go back every year and be the same person, but you'll always be re-enacting a lie. You won't be nearly as close to those old friends or family members, because they'll never actually know the real you. You won't feel connected. You need them to love your actual self, or they won't be loving you. They'll be loving a fake memory of you.

This goes for all of your relationships. When your root chakra is closed off, you won't feel any control. You won't feel like you belong or like you deserve to be part of a community. You need to explore those feelings, enter that energy and open it up. You need to allow your relationships to thrive, and the only way to do this is through self-acceptance and self-love.

Don't be what others want you to be. Be yourself.

I also see a lot of relationship problems that stem from birth energy. We are all endowed with an energy when we're born.[xi] However, very few births are perfect, and thus we're left with this imperfect energy after delivery. If that energy isn't treated, it can affect us throughout our lives.

Any hitch in your birth can cause problems in your birth energy. If you were born early or late, you'll always feel like you're just a little bit off your time line. If you were a breech birth, you may always feel like you are at the wrong place at the wrong time. If your mother struggled to deliver you, you might find yourself having small struggles with people all of the time.

For instance, let's consider what happens if you are born later than expected, or after an induced labor. Perhaps you'll find that your relationships end because people get tired of you, just like your mother got tired of carrying on her pregnancy. Maybe you feel like you're not ready for certain milestones in your life, but they come along anyway. Perhaps it feels like you're rushed through things, and your needs never come first.

Whatever your individual case, it's important to get birth energy cleared up. Your root chakra will thank you for turning that birth energy into something useful and supportive. Work on visualizing an idealized birth scenario, and keep it handy.

Take The FREE 3-Minute Chakra Healing Test. Find out how each of your 7 Chakras may be influencing your health and life

www.VelocityHousePresents.com/chakrahealing   **21**

Connect with your infantile self, in order to manipulate your birth energy into something healthier. Visualize the "perfect birth," and shape your birth energy into that form. Imagine that your mother carried you until you were ready and that the delivery itself was smooth and quick. Once you were "born," imagine the love and acceptance from your waiting parents and relatives. This will get you back on the right time line and reset your birth energy to a healthier state. Whenever your birth energy feels off, just re-visualize that perfect birth, and your root chakra will realign to that ideal. Your birth energy will become something that supports and helps you through life, instead of something that constantly works against you.

Your birth energy is very hard to reset over the long term, but constantly revisiting your "new birth" will establish a good habit. Get rid of all that baggage from your birth, and don't let it hinder you any longer.

Again, I feel it's important to mention that your root chakra could be suffering from any combination of money, health, and relationship issues. They're not mutually exclusive in any way. In each of the three sections, I listed some very specific methods you can employ to reconnect with the specific aspect of issues your root chakra is exhibiting. If you are suffering from multiple deficiencies, however, or if you can't seem to connect to your root chakra, there are also simple and efficient methods you can utilize to improve your overall connection with your root chakra.

One of the most elegant exercises involves the connection between your root chakra and your foot chakra. As I said in the last chapter, the foot chakra is a large source of energy for you to tap into. However, that energy can't do any good if it's blocked. It's like a wall outlet with nothing in it. The power is there, but it's waiting for something to connect to it.

I want you to use the exact visualization of plugging into a wall outlet to connect your root chakra to your foot chakra. Your root chakra is right in your groin and tailbone area. Now imagine that your spinal cord doesn't end around your tailbone. Imagine that it in fact hangs out of your tailbone, like a wire. Take that wire and plug it into your foot chakra. Feel the live current rushing from the foot chakra into your root chakra. Can you feel all of the energy you now have access to? Put it to use in your dealings with money, in your pursuit of good health, in your relationships. Let them thrive.

Take The FREE 3-Minute Chakra Healing Test. Find out how each of your 7 Chakras may be influencing your health and life

22   www.VelocityHousePresents.com/chakrahealing

It's going to take practice. Your foot chakra isn't a great outlet. It's one of those old, loose outlets where the plug occasionally slips out of the wall. You might go days without any problems, only for the plug to slip out randomly. When it does, just plug it back in. Keep the energy flowing. This great exercise is similar to "Just look down at your feet." It's a low-effort, easily-maintained exercise that you can do no matter where you are.

When you're at home and really want to work on strengthening your root chakra, however, you can try out a more intense exercise. Now, we're going to clear out the old energy from your root chakra. Remember earlier when we visualized and located our root chakra? It's a molten ball of lead right in your groin area, in the center of your hips. Focus on that red-hot energy again, the snake coiled around it, and try to hold that image in your mind. Once the image is stable, go into your root chakra, and see where you are wounded. Maybe it's bad birth energy or maybe an unbalance. Maybe you can picture the wounds that are causing your relationships strife or you are holding on to extra weight. These wounds will look like dark blotches on the surface of your beautiful, red energy.

Just like with our foot chakra, this blotchy energy will feel uncomfortable. It's supposed to feel uncomfortable. That's how we know we're in the right spot. Now dump that bad energy. Scoop it out by the handful and dump it on the ground. Get rid of it. Let it be absorbed back into the Earth from whence it came. As you do so, I recommend stating to yourself what the problem is. For example:

"I'm releasing this energy. I can never hold onto my money. I am bad at handling my finances. I spend money needlessly. I waste money. I am foolish with cash. I can't be responsible. I will not amount to anything if I keep up these habits."

Take all of that, and get rid of it. Throw it out. It's not helping you. Now think of that beautiful red energy again, of the snake and the lead and the earth that embodies your root chakra. Use those to fill the empty space you created. You don't want to leave your root chakra with no energy. You don't want to leave it barren. That allows all sorts of chaos to enter the space. Instead, fill your root chakra with the new energy. Fill it with the correct color. Turn it into a haven for your snake or whatever personalized animal lives in your root chakra. Make it into

Take The FREE 3-Minute Chakra Healing Test. Find out how each of your 7 Chakras may be influencing your health and life

www.VelocityHousePresents.com/chakrahealing   23

a safe place, aligned with your body's needs. Heal those wounds by replacing the tainted energy with the correct energy.

This may take several efforts, especially if you're new to this type of energy manipulation, but I love this because it's very clean and very gentle. There's no destruction going on here. We're not destroying energy. We acknowledge that the bad energy isn't right for us, but then we return it to the Earth so others can use it. Then we bring in the energy we need for nourishing our personal root chakra. We accept ourselves as individuals.

Let the energy flow from your foot chakra into your root chakra and heal those age-old worries. Stop just surviving or just getting by. Allow yourself to thrive in terms of money, health, and relationships. Once that's done, and you've filled the whole space with a healthier and more positive energy, we're ready for something more erotic: the sacral chakra, home to our body's sexual energies.

Take The FREE 3-Minute Chakra Healing Test. Find out how each of your 7 Chakras may be influencing your health and life

24   *www.VelocityHousePresents.com/chakrahealing*

CHAPTER 4

Chakra Two:
The Sacral Chakra

Where the foot chakra keeps us grounded in the world at large, and the root chakra concerns the roles we play in a community, the sacral chakra deals with our more personal relationships. The sacral chakra contains a very primal, raw form of sexual energy that we can also use as a creative force, provided we're equipped to do so.[xii] If you aren't equipped to do so, you might be like my client Rich. He had many friends, plenty of money, a steady job...but he couldn't perform in bed anymore. He was closed off. He even told me he "resented" sex, though he had no idea why. He didn't get the point anymore.

It was causing him real pain. Here's this 26-year-old guy, and he couldn't figure out why he had these feelings. By all rights, he knew he should be out there with his peers, having fun and enjoying himself, but instead, he was actively avoiding situations where he had to put himself out there. He steered clear of anything that could end in a potential hookup. He was confused and frustrated.

I wasted no time. I asked him if he'd been through any sexual traumas recently. At first, he was hesitant, but he finally admitted that he and his long-time girlfriend had split up a few months back in a nasty breakup. It was one of those breakups where things are thrown, hateful things are screamed across war-zone living rooms, and friendships are lost— a total mess. In the course of it all, the girl had made some comments about Rich that hurt his sexual energy. It wounded him. He felt objectified; he felt hurt, and he felt unloved.

If any part of Rich's narrative sounds familiar, it's likely that you're also dealing with a wounded sacral chakra. The sacral chakra is very fragile, because sexuality is such an insecure or vulnerable part of our lives. It's very easy to damage. Luckily, it's also resilient.

An opened sacral chakra is a beautiful thing. As I said, this isn't just about sexuality. This is about sexuality as a creative force of energy that you can tap into. Don't get me wrong; sex is definitely part of it. An open sacral chakra creates healthy, tender sexual experiences with people who respect you.

There's more to it than sex, though. An open sacral chakra adds something to all of your creative endeavors. It manifests as this raw, primal undercurrent in all your work. You're going to recognize this power and fire in everything that you do. The sacral chakra wants to infiltrate every aspect of your life. It wants you to take advantage of that energy reserve. It's not that you need to be sexy all of the time in order to feel loved—your sexuality will be a natural part of your creative process, and it will shine through automatically.

It just happens that our most obvious warning signs when dealing with the sacral chakra arise in our sex drives. You might not notice that you aren't taking advantage of your sexual energies in your work, but you'll surely notice if your sex life dries up.

In fact, by the time you're actively having problems in your sex life your sacral chakra is probably very damaged. Unfortunately, it's quite normal for people to ignore the creative energies of their sacral chakra. This displays a slight neglect of the sacral chakra. A failed sex drive, however, shows a sacral chakra under siege and you must address this immediately.

You may also notice problems in your sacral chakra through the corresponding parts of your body. The sacral chakra is responsible for the health of your reproductive system and your bladder—anything in your lower abdomen, really—and your hips.[xiii] If you're having health

Take The FREE 3-Minute Chakra Healing Test. Find out how each of your 7 Chakras may be influencing your health and life

26   www.VelocityHousePresents.com/chakrahealing

problems in any of these areas, it's a good idea to check on your sacral chakra; chances are that it's also sick.

One last thing: be careful of addictions masquerading as love. Love is persistent in all of the chakras, but I often work with clients who are convinced that the sacral chakra is "more responsible" for love. Their image of love is all mixed up with sex and sexuality, and that's a very dangerous road to go down. It presents love in an adulterated form, instead of the pure energy source we should be taking advantage of.

In the past, society was built on hierarchies. We loved to put things on pedestals, to develop rankings and to invest in authorities. Now, however, our society is more egalitarian. We are in the Aquarian Era of energy, which values support and friendship. Peers are more important than authority figures. Addictions are a remnant of the hierarchies of the past. You're putting whatever you're addicted to above your own needs.

Your chakra is likely hurt if you carry around addictions, and you should clear them out or transform them into some other, more positive type of energy as soon as possible. It's not that hierarchies are innately bad, but our experience is constantly shifting. The chakras thrive in an environment of equality; each of them being in a balanced state. Try to remember this whenever possible. Don't be addicted to sex-as-love. Allow yourself to experience love, period. This is much healthier and has a smaller chance of negative repercussions.

Let's check in with your sacral chakra right now. The sacral chakra is located in the middle of your stomach (and the corresponding spot on your back), approximately two or three finger-widths above the root chakra. Traditionally, it's associated with the color orange, the element fire, the metal tin and the jaguar.[xiv] I especially like the use of orange and fire, as I've always thought of the sacral chakra as a warm fireplace, full of energy in my stomach. As always, if you don't like any of these traditional choices, you're free to choose your own. This is *your* chakra.

Now focus on your sacral chakra. Focus on that orange fireplace in your abdomen, a jaguar curled up next to it. Feel it? Rate how open your sacral chakra feels on a zero-to-ten point scale. A zero would be close to my client Rich, cut off from his sexuality and extremely frustrated. A ten would mean that your sacral chakra is an open pool of energy you can draw from regularly.

Take The FREE 3-Minute Chakra Healing Test. Find out how each of your 7 Chakras may be influencing your health and life

www.VelocityHousePresents.com/chakrahealing   **27**

The best part about the sacral chakra is that reconnecting and healing its energy is so much fun. In fact, the sacral chakra is my favorite to work on, because it simply requires pampering your primal, lustful side.

These are some examples I've used in the past to help people reconnect to their sacral chakra: long warm showers, highly self-indulgent meals (lots of steak and chocolate), walks by the beach, candlelight, massages, and sex (especially sex with attention to the spiritual aspects, as in tantric sex), to name a few.[xv]

The key to connecting to your sacral chakra is spoiling yourself. The reason is quite simple: when you indulge, you'll feel the energy in your sacral chakra react. This trains your body to recognize this energy source in the future, allowing you to draw upon it as needed.

Treat yourself and your body. Get in touch with that primal energy that resides inside of you. Nourish it. Give your sacral chakra something to work with. Relax and let it take over for a while. Free yourself to indulge occasionally, and you'll find that your sacral chakra flourishes. It's easy and fun, so there's really no excuse *not* to be in contact with your sacral chakra.

I also find it's helpful to start my day by allowing pleasure into my life and greeting it. When I feel like I'm growing a bit distant from my sacral chakra, I like to start my day by welcoming pleasure: something along the lines of, "Today, something will happen that I find pleasurable and take joy from." This simple statement sets the Law of Attraction to work. As long as I have an uninterrupted flow of energy from my foot chakra to my sacral chakra, manifesting pleasure throughout the course of the day should be easy. I'm attracting this primal, sexual energy into my life.

If you're dealing with old wounds in your sacral chakra, however, you must clear out the old energy before you can fully heal. In that case, we're going to do an exercise very similar to what we did with our root chakra.

Using your flattened hand, I want you to begin tapping on your stomach at a steady pace, right where your sacral chakra is located. This will help you focus on your sacral chakra and begin stirring the energy kept within. If you've ever done any tapping exercises before, this should be familiar.

Take The FREE 3-Minute Chakra Healing Test. Find out how each of your 7 Chakras may be influencing your health and life

28   *www.VelocityHousePresents.com/chakrahealing*

From there, you will start repeating clearing statements. You want to speak out loud the intention to purge your energy center. For instance, you could start with:

"I'm going to clear this old energy. I'm allowing my sacral chakra to clean itself. I'm letting go of these negative feelings. I'm letting go of this anger and this frustration. I'm allowing myself to feel pleasure. I'm allowing myself to love sex. I'm letting go of what's holding me back. I am ready to heal. I embrace sexuality and pleasure."

Anything along these lines can work. Just say whatever is honestly on your mind or whatever you feel is holding you back. Be specific. Instruct your chakra on what you need to clear out. Tell your chakra how to heal. As you go on, you'll probably find your brain steering you towards new clearing statements. Your brain already subconsciously knows what's wrong. The initial clearing statements will help you lose your inhibitions, allowing your true feelings to come out. Express these new clearing statements aloud. Let them out.

I also find that blinking helps with the clearing process; scientists think blinking helps us refocus our thoughts.[xvi] Blink rhythmically while you say the clearing statements, and help your brain reset your neural pathways into new, healthy energy patterns.

Once you've done that, proceed like we did with the root chakra. Picture the fireplace in your stomach once again. Can you see where the bad energy is? Can you see where it's unhealthy? Maybe it's places where your fireplace isn't burning quite as brightly or has gone out entirely.

Scoop that old energy out, like it is ashes and charred logs. Put it back into the ground where it belongs. Of course, that might not clear it all out. Now concentrate on your sacral chakra. Remember how I said earlier that I like to think of the sacral chakra as a little furnace? We're going to turn our furnace on and burn away any remnants of that bad energy. Think of it like turning the oven on, and that meal that spilled on the bottom last night is just burning off, leaving your oven nice and clean. Heat your sacral chakra up so it burns away that old, wounded energy. Then take a deep breath, filling your sacral chakra back up with clean, pure energy. Repeat as many times as necessary until your sacral chakra is clear and open.

Sexual abuse as a child also affects the sacral chakra and has its own associated technique for clearing. Sexual abuse is exceedingly tough to address, and the scars are deep, so we have to be careful how we heal such a sensitive area of the chakra.

In my experience, the most effective method is communicating with your inner child. Your inner child isn't just a saying or a figment of your imagination. It's a real force in your body, and it needs nourishment and love. It's a piece of your childhood psyche and emotions which resides forever in you, even as you move into adulthood—a part of your youth that you subconsciously cling to and consult.

Your inner child holds those scars from abuse, and you need to help him or her move past them. Grab a journal and write to your inner child. Say hello. Say that you understand what happened was not okay.

Then, switch hands. Put your pen in your non-dominant hand, where your handwriting is probably worse—it will look more like a child's handwriting. Let your inner child write. Let him or her talk about emotions and anger and frustrations. Just let him or her take over and communicate with you. You're letting your higher faculties go away for a while, letting your subconscious mind take over and address the problem. Give your inner child a voice.

This is your sacral chakra at work. Your sacral chakra is working to clear out these negative energies through this journal exercise. Your inner child is demanding to be heard instead of being ignored. Ignoring your childhood self all this time has caused the wound fester. You've repressed the pain, but not in a healthy way. The wound is infected. Let it all come out. I urged you earlier to utilize clearing statements in helping you connect to your chakras. This process—letting your inner child write out its problems—is allowing your inner child to take advantage of clearing statements. Your inner child is literally helping your sacral chakra know what to clear by expressing its emotions. Let it clear. As you work, fuse your inner child and your adult self. You're not two parts of a whole; you inhabit the same body, and you share the same energies. Embrace and accept the emotions of your inner child. Doing so will help your inner child clear your sacral chakra so you both can be at peace.

You might have to do this over a long period. I filled four or five notebooks using this tactic. Letting out your childhood anger and

Take The FREE 3-Minute Chakra Healing Test. Find out how each of your 7 Chakras may be influencing your health and life

30   www.VelocityHousePresents.com/chakrahealing

sadness is a very freeing experience. I think you'll be surprised how much you've been holding back. When you're done freeing your inner child, set them next to your sacral chakra. Put him or her right next to that warm, comfortable energy source and show love.

Little John Lake is doing much better these days. He's well-adjusted, he's nourished, and he's supported. I don't need to struggle against him anymore.

My client Rich is doing well, also. Within a few weeks of our first session, I had him back in the dating world. A year or so after that, I was proud to go to his wedding. Nowadays he's a thriving father of two children, satisfied and comfortable with his life. Getting in touch with his sacral chakra also led to an interest in painting, which he continues to do to this day. Really primal stuff. Very impressive.

Even though too many people live with a stunted sacral chakra or live disconnected from that primal energy, that doesn't mean you have to. Clear out all your old wounds and all your tainted energy. Let your sacral chakra flourish. You'll be amazed at the results.

Take The FREE 3-Minute Chakra Healing Test. Find out how each of your 7 Chakras may be influencing your health and life

www.VelocityHousePresents.com/chakrahealing

31

CHAPTER 5

Chakra Three: Navel Chakra

Power. That's the centerpiece of the navel chakra.

Power is a curious concept, because so few people have it, but so many people *think* they have it. So many people emulate the outward trappings of power, without understanding what power actually is.

As a depressed twenty-something, I thought power meant control. I felt powerless already. I felt like a victim of circumstances much larger than myself. I saw my life slipping by with no plans and nothing good coming of it, and I felt helpless to fix any of my problems. As a result, I became incredibly controlling. I micromanaged anything I had even a modicum of control over. One of the first people I drove out of my life was my significant other.

I had a great girlfriend. We'd met towards the end of college, moved in together once we graduated and got along great for a few years. Unfortunately, as my depression and apathy spread, I began to neglect our relationship. I withdrew into myself and stopped providing her the love and support she needed. She responded in kind; I felt her drawing away. I couldn't see that I was at fault, so I felt like she was abandoning the relationship. I began exerting control over her, desperate to reconcile. I demanded to know where she was at all times. I was afraid when she went to work, because I didn't have control anymore. We stopped going out, stopped visiting friends and stopped doing anything that I couldn't tightly oversee. She left me.

Once she left, my control issues only got worse, and spread to other areas of my life. I tried to control my few remaining friends; I tried to control my food intake; I tried to control my habits. I controlled everything I could get my hands on. This sounds like what you'd do if you had power, right? Power means being in control.

Yes and no. People who have power will occasionally find themselves in control, but they don't define themselves by what they control. Control is actually the opposite of power. It's a substitute for real power. Control is really a fear of being powerless.[xvii]

If you fear that you're powerless in your relationships, you become controlling. You start demanding to know where your girlfriend or boyfriend is at all hours of the night. You obsess over the smallest details. In other words, you become a nightmare.

This extends to all aspects of your life. Control is the man who's sliding over a cliff, desperately holding on by his fingertips. Control is a last resort. It's a result of desperation, not power.

Picture the Mississippi or Colorado River. A river is powerful. It's just water, but it's immensely powerful. The water doesn't try to "control" its surroundings. The surroundings get out of the way of the river. The river's course seems natural. Sometimes the river is calm and quiet, other times the water is thrashing. Regardless, the river follows its course. The river's path is determined and sure; it twists and turns around obstacles in its path, always continuing along its established channel.

It makes sense, therefore, that the navel chakra is embodied by the element water. The navel chakra is a reservoir of energy in your upper abdomen, right around your solar plexus, and is responsible for keeping you from feeling victimized or helpless.[xviii] It holds your self-esteem. It's what keeps you solid and determined in life.

Like every chakra, the navel chakra corresponds to various parts of your body. In this case, the liver, pancreas, gallbladder, and lower back all fall under the dominion of the navel chakra. If you're having health

Take The FREE 3-Minute Chakra Healing Test. Find out how each of your 7 Chakras may be influencing your health and life

34   www.VelocityHousePresents.com/chakrahealing

issues with any of these areas, it's likely that you need to examin your relationship with power. Some of these body parts even correspond to specific problems with your chakra.

The naval chakra is associated with the color yellow, the metal iron and the hummingbird animal totem.[xix] Now, you might have your own animal totem. Maybe you want something more aggressive in this spot— say, a mountain lion or a tiger. You're free to explore different options. I do think that the hummingbird is great here, though, because it is the opposite of what you'd expect. It really displays perfectly why the navel chakra is different than our traditional understanding of power.

The hummingbird isn't a fierce animal. It's not an animal we think of as a fearsome or aggressive. It pollinates. It hovers. It flies backward if it wants. For its size, it's very powerful, but it's still not a predatory animal. The hummingbird is a perfect partner to the naval chakra, because it shows what kind of power we're dealing with. This is a quiet, understated power. This is a calming power, just like the ocean or the river. It's an undercurrent, not the overt focus.

Personally, I like the idea of the hummingbird. I like its symbolism. If you contact your navel chakra and find a different representative animal, however, go with what is true for you. This is your chakra.

Let's get in touch with our navel chakra right now. Focus on that area of your upper abdomen, right around your solar plexus, and feel the energy there. Now measure how open and connected you feel to your navel chakra, with a one meaning that you're completely closed off and a ten meaning your chakra is entirely open and useful.

If you're feeling closed off from your navel chakra, you must figure out why. Most of the time, people who are disconnected from their navel chakra are actually giving their power away. It's not that they have no power; it's that they've invested that power in other things.

If you read the chapter on the sacral chakra, you might remember my discussion concerning love versus addiction. Addictions often feel like love, but they're really a substitute. Similarly, we tend to find substitutes for power, and that is where we place the focus of our energies, neglecting our navel chakra in the process.

Take a minute and think about power. Grab a pen and paper, if you'd like, and list off all the things you associate with power.

Some common ideas about power I hear from clients are: money, sex, control, bossing people around, and knowledge.

These are just surrogates for power. Worse, when you associate these ideas with power, you allow them power over you. For instance, I often hear people associate money and power. It's one of the most widespread misconceptions. The problem is that you're giving money control over your life. You're letting money stop you. So many people suffer from lower back issues—tightness, soreness, twinges. Pain in your lower back is actually a sign that you give money too much power. They are directly correlated.

What do I mean by "giving money power"? When is the last time you wanted something and then said, "But I can't afford that." You're letting money dictate the way you live. You're giving money power over your life. That's no good! Money is a tool. Money is an aid. Money is not power. Would you let a hammer have power over your life? How about a chainsaw? Of course not. Money is the same.

Take charge of your own life. My father always used to say, "You're a smart kid. If you *really* wanted that thing, you'd find a way to make it work." The same goes for you. If you want something, *really* want something, nothing can stop you: not money, not relationships, not bosses, nothing. That's where the navel chakra comes into play. You can't let outside forces dictate your actions. You can't let outside forces stop the *wanting*. Instead, acknowledge your desire and then start working towards it.

When your navel chakra is closed off, you will feel like a victim to these various entities. You will feel like a lack of money is holding you back in life and has power over you, or that your relationships are preventing you from living your own life. When you take back your power, your self-confidence and your self-esteem, you will be able to trust yourself and keep moving forward.

Others give power away in their relationships. They become what others want them to be. They let others dictate the way they live and fear communicating their own needs. Many times this isn't an active choice; they think that people will like them more if they aim to please all the time or if they don't rock the boat.

In doing so, they close off their navel chakra and their situation worsens. Others might not be mad at them, but they will struggle to

Take The FREE 3-Minute Chakra Healing Test. Find out how each of your 7 Chakras may be influencing your health and life

36   www.VelocityHousePresents.com/chakrahealing

make close friends. If you don't open up to people and act like a distinct, unique human being, you aren't actually being a great friend. You're not being honest.

Giving away power has an effect on the quality of your life, as well. You're passing up on opportunities, because you think that you're not worthy, or that others need them more. While "selfish" has bad connotations, sometimes looking after yourself is necessary. You deserve success. You deserve happiness. Claim your power. Take it back.

The navel chakra is a lot like the sacral chakra, in that it's *fun* to reconnect. There are the standard energy manipulations that we can use (more on those later in the chapter), but we can also have a lot of fun. Our aim is aggression. Take our power back by force.

We're going to get in touch with our primal side. Be a warrior. Go into a safe place and yell. Give out a huge war cry. Get excited. Break out of your patterns. Break some plates against a wall. Do something crazy that embraces that primitive side and gets your adrenaline pumping. Get in touch with this power inside of you.

It doesn't need to be a huge act. Try simply changing your routine every day. We like routines, because we like controlling our day. Don't let yourself fall into patterns of behavior anymore; introduce something new so that your energy is constantly shifting. Going for a hike always makes me feel powerful—connecting to nature while simultaneously conquering my body.

There are so many ways to connect to your navel chakra; you don't really have an excuse *not* to. Whether you're loud and aggressive like ocean breakers, or calm and subdued like the Mississippi River, you can easily get in touch with this third chakra.

I do find it helpful to clear out any old energy, though. Even once we reconnect to our navel chakra, it is still helpful to ensure it's running at full efficiency. For this, we use more traditional energy manipulations.

In this exercise, tap on what we call the "Karate Chop Point."[xx] That's the fleshy side of your hand, the part that you would use if you were going to chop a board in half. Use two fingers of one hand to tap on the Karate Chop Point of the other (doesn't matter which hand plays each role). As we tap, we're going to use something called setup statements to purge our old energy. Setup statements consist of two parts: an acknowledgment of the problem, followed by an acceptance.

"Even though I give my power away too often, I'm ready to change that. Even though I've given my power to others, I am ready to reclaim it. Even though I have been controlling in the past, I am ready to improve. Even though I have tried so hard to please others, I'm ready to look after my own needs, for once."

Try writing some of your own that are more specific to your own situation. Remember, it's an acknowledgment of the problem followed by an acceptance of the problem and a willingness to move past it.

As you work, you should feel the energies stirring. Once you've identified the breadth of the problem, reach in and remove those bad energies. Release them back into the ground, and fill your navel chakra with new, clean energy. Immediately after you clear out the old energy, do some of those aggressive exercises we discussed earlier. Break some plates or do some primal screaming. Let that new, pure energy rush in and fill the void we just left.

Then think about the people you interact with daily. Imagine how you will deal with them now. Don't let your old, powerless self take hold again. Draw upon your navel chakra and imagine your next conversation with those people. Be your new self. Revel in your power, whether it's aggressive or subdued.

You've now cleared all three of your lower chakras: the root, the sacral, and the navel. Now we will move into the more abstract ones, starting with the heart chakra.

Take The FREE 3-Minute Chakra Healing Test. Find out how each of your 7 Chakras may be influencing your health and life

38   *www.VelocityHousePresents.com/chakrahealing*

CHAPTER 6

Chakra Four:
The Heart Chakra

Your chakras are like a large circuit, running through your body. Just like your circulatory system begins and ends at your heart, your chakras are all connected.[xxi] This is important, because it establishes continuity. Our lower three chakras—root, sacral, and navel—are just as important as our higher chakras. A blockage in our lower chakras will hurt our higher chakras and vice versa. However, our upper chakras do have one unique feature: they are responsible for "tutoring" our lower chakras. Only with the help of our upper chakras can we raise our lower chakras into healthier, higher vibration levels. Thus, it's important that we immediately remedy any issues in our upper chakras, keeping this flow unimpeded.

The upper four chakras begin with the heart chakra, which (as you probably guessed) is located at our heart. It's responsible for directing the flow of energy from our lower chakras to our higher ones. Our heart is an organ, yes, but it's also intelligent. When we open our fourth chakra, we keep the entire system flowing correctly. The heart chakra is traditionally associated with the eagle, the element air, and the metal copper, as well as the color green.[xxii] As always, you're free to personalize your chakra's color and animal totem depending on your preferences.

There's a Beatles song that says, "And in the end, the love you take is equal to the love you make."[xxiii] I think they must have been very in-tune with their heart chakras, because that's pretty much what the heart chakra asks of us. An open heart chakra means that we find love within ourselves, and that's all the love we need to keep going. Any love we receive from the outside is just a bonus.

I used to have a really hard time with this. I was always seeking approval from people. I wanted people to like me. It's a natural tendency, wanting people to like us! We're communal creatures. Unfortunately, that got in the way of my own happiness. I kept looking to others for acceptance. I kept looking outwards for love. However, the only way people will love you, is if you first love yourself.

Then, you must accept that everyone loves differently. Some people are very open about love. They give hugs and kisses; they call on your birthday, and they shower you with gifts. Those are great people, and we all recognize how loving they are. Others won't, though. They're not very physical people; they might not call you *ever* (let alone on your birthday), and you'll never hear them say those three magic words. The trouble is recognizing that those are also people who love you equally.

It's difficult recognizing when we have closed off from our heart chakra. I had a client whose relationship with her father was along these lines. She wanted so much for him to love her, but he was a more traditional archetype of a man. He adhered firmly to older gender roles. He wasn't very outwardly affectionate; he was a bit gruff when he spoke, and he rarely shed a tear.

It was only after we opened my client's heart chakra that she realized her father *did* love her, but in his own special way. He would never be the dad who was "there for her" or who called to check up on her. He might never say "I love you" out loud to my client. It wasn't in his nature, and she just had to accept that. Once she did, it seemed like her relationship with her father was completely different. She understood him, regardless of the fact that she lived her life a different way. Furthermore, she didn't *need* his love anymore. Her love came from inside, sustaining her and keeping her strong.

When we close off our heart chakra, it's like we're addicted to love, and we want to experience it in our own particular way. We sustain

Take The FREE 3-Minute Chakra Healing Test. Find out how each of your 7 Chakras may be influencing your health and life

40   www.VelocityHousePresents.com/chakrahealing

ourselves off of other people's love. We're parasites, of a sort. We feel that pleasing others will make us feel loved. It makes it difficult to commit to any relationship. It should come as no surprise that this disconnect is often due to heartbreak.

A few years back, I had a great relationship in which I was content and comfortable. Throughout the relationship, I felt very connected to my heart chakra and felt a lot of love for myself. When we broke up, that was the first thing to go. I walled up my heart. Commitment to anyone or anything else was difficult for months afterward. It was just too painful; my heart chakra felt too raw. I'm a professional, and I'll still be the first to admit that the heart chakra is fragile. It's very easily hurt, and it's very easy to succumb to the "illusion" of heartbreak.

I say illusion simply because the heart is never truly broken. It's becomes closed off and needs to be reopened so that we can experience love again in all its glory. It's *easy* to close off your heart chakra, but it's similarly easy to open it back up, provided you know how.

Take a moment and rate your connection to your heart chakra. A zero indicates you're completely closed off, meaning you probably have a hard time committing to relationships, and you try to please others in order to gain their love. If you've been through heartbreak recently, it's likely that you're closer to this end of the scale, unfortunately.

If your heart is open, you're in a much better place. You're committed, or at least find it easy to commit yourself. You're connected to others. Most importantly, you recognize that you can love yourself. You need not turn to an outside source for love. Being loved by others is fantastic. It feels great, and you can build a great relationship when both people love each other. However, all the love you *need* comes from inside you. You don't need anyone else. As long as you love yourself, you're perfect.

Then, you can share that love with others. You won't run out of love, so no worries there. You're free to give your love to others, without worrying about whether they reciprocate. You don't need to feel sorry for them if they aren't connected to their heart chakra or if they find it hard to commit. Instead, you accept them. You recognize their uniqueness, and you love them anyway.

This is also the essence of true forgiveness. It stems from acknowledging that you were wronged, but you continue to love the person

Take The FREE 3-Minute Chakra Healing Test. Find out how each of your 7 Chakras may be influencing your health and life

www.VelocityHousePresents.com/chakrahealing   **41**

who wronged you in spite of it. It's not a mental switch that you flip; it's your heart chakra's energies realigning, which allow for forgiveness. It's hard to reach this point, but it's worthwhile.

Luckily, there are many ways for us to open up our heart chakra. The first is a very simple technique. You can do it at home, at work and practically anywhere. It doesn't require much time or effort. All it requires is your focus. Concentrate on your heart chakra. Put your hand over your heart, right above that energy center. It's almost as if you were saying the Pledge of Allegiance. Stay focused and repeat the words: "I'm okay, no matter what happens."

Alter the wording as you go, narrowing your focus. "I feel loved, no matter what happens," or, "I have all the love I need and that comforts me." Use anything that plays off of the theme that you are loved and the love you receive arises internally. Repeat it as long as you feel is necessary.

This repetition technique is good for settling your heart chakra. If you've recently taken a light wound to your heart chakra or feel like it's restless, repeating "I'm okay no matter what happens," can help calm down the energy and realign it into healthy patterns. You might need to work more with the wounded energy later, but this technique can at least start the healing process and stop things from becoming more aggravated.

Another great technique I take advantage of regularly is the, "It feels scary because..." pattern. When you close off your heart chakra, it might feel like you've walled it up. You've built this fortress around your heart to keep it safe. An open heart chakra recognizes that these walls are unnecessary and, in fact, harmful.

We use the "It feels scary because..." method to get in touch with our feelings. Place your hand on your heart again, and finish the sentence. Why does it feel scary to tear down the walls around your heart? What is holding you back?

"It feels scary, because someone could hurt me. It feels scary, because I'm afraid to open up. It feels scary, because I don't like commitments. It feels scary, because people might not love me as much as I love them."

You need to comfort your scared self. Tell yourself it's safe—that you don't need to rely on anyone else for love. Accept yourself. I find visualization is a great complement to this technique. Just as we've done

Take The FREE 3-Minute Chakra Healing Test. Find out how each of your 7 Chakras may be influencing your health and life

42   www.VelocityHousePresents.com/chakrahealing

with the other chakras, picture the energy in your heart chakra. Imagine your heart as a glowing ball of light, too bright for others to even look at. It's like you have a miniature sun in your chest.

Once you have a clear vision of your heart chakra, straining with light, begin tapping on your chest with the palm of your hand. As you do so, begin releasing your fears.

"I am clearing this old energy from my heart chakra. I am ready to love myself. I am ready to give others my love. I'm not afraid that others will hurt me, because I believe in myself. I refuse to be heartbroken. My heart is open and ready to receive this energy. I am ready to commit. I am ready to love and be loved."

Clear that old energy out of your heart chakra. Watch it flow out of you and back into the ground. Then push more energy into your heart chakra. If there are walls around your heart chakra, you'll see them bulge outward. You'll see your heart chakra straining against those bonds, the eagle desperately seeking freedom. Keep filling your heart chakra with more energy until those walls can't take it anymore.

Watch the walls explode, your heart chakra shining out in all its glory, the eagle bursting from its cage. Notice that it doesn't feel hurt. It feels safe. It feels warm. It feels joyous. Then, wall it back up. That's right, build those walls around your heart again. Close it off. Notice how dim everything feels. Notice how stunted your emotions feel.

Start filling your heart with energy again. Push it up against the walls of the box one more time, until the box blows open again. Look inside the box at your heart, and see that it's okay. It's undamaged. Repeat this as many times as you'd like, until you're satisfied that your heart can't be hurt. It can't be damaged unless you let it. As long as you keep your heart full of positive energy, you'll be fine.

Open your heart. It's the central conduit that spreads energy from your lower chakras to your upper chakras, and it's vital that this channel remain open. When you're satisfied that your heart chakra is routing energy correctly, you're ready to move on.

CHAPTER 7

Chakra Five:
Throat Chakra

Have you ever seen the film *The King's Speech*?[xxiv]

The plot of the film follows (with a bit of artistic license) the life story of English monarch, King George VI, who suffered from a terrible stutter and fear of public speaking. He begins seeing a speech therapist in order to get over his ailment, training relentlessly to eliminate his stutter and confront a national audience. Poor King George. If only he'd been more in touch with his throat chakra.

Sure, *The King's Speech* is an extreme example of what can happen when your throat chakra is closed off, but it definitely sums up the problem. Our throat chakra, the fifth, is responsible for governing our speech. As such, it corresponds to the throat, thyroid, vocal cords, jaw, mouth and neck.[xxv] Any illnesses you encounter with this part of the body stem from an imbalance in your throat chakra. For instance, an abundance of sore throats normally signals a neglected throat chakra.

The throat chakra also covers any mental issues that affect speech. It's not just a physical problem. Stuttering, a fear of public speaking or a habitual failure to speak up for yourself are all caused by a closed off throat chakra. Maybe you find expressing your feelings to your family;

for fear that they will judge you. Instead, you keep your mouth shut and close off from everyone around you. You fail to tell your spouse what you want—what you *need*—because silence seems safer.

Maybe you have a problem at work? Are you sabotaging your career, because you never stand out? You know the answers; you know how to help your boss, but you're afraid to speak up. You don't want to draw attention to yourself. This simultaneously hurts your company and your own prospects; your boss will pass over you for a promotion, because you haven't proven your worth.

It's as if someone is choking you. You may not be physically choking—your throat might be clear, your vocal cords ready to speak, but your throat chakra is choked. Every once in a while you manage to say something, but overall you're silent. You can't express yourself. You know that it's wrong, and that speaking up would help everyone, but something is holding you back.

Even when you do speak, you can't speak the truth. You're afraid to express your needs or say what you want. You go along with others, because you don't want to provoke conflict. You feel weak and stymied in your attempts to talk to people. You feel like nobody will listen even if you do get a word in. It's difficult not being able to communicate.

On the flip side, an open throat chakra is pretty easy to surmise. You're very open and talkative, though not just "chatty." You speak with purpose; you're strong and affirm your needs. You're not afraid to upset others, because you know that you speak truth. Others listen, because they recognize the strength of your character. You easily and habitually express yourself and give your thoughts purpose.

Before we go further, let's check in with your throat chakra. Your throat chakra is traditionally sapphire blue in color, though your personal color might be different.[xxvi] There's no animal totem this time, as we move into the upper realms, but we do still have an element (ether) and a metal (mercury). We're moving out of the physical realm and into the spiritual, inner realm. Still, if you do picture an animal totem in conjunction with your throat chakra, that experience is not wrong. It's unique, and it's personal.

Take a moment and envision a reservoir of sapphire blue energy liquid mercury nestled in the hollow of your throat. How open does that energy feel? How healthy is your connection to your throat chakra? Rate your connection on a zero-to-ten scale. A zero means that your throat chakra is completely closed off, while a ten means you're fully in control of that energy and draw upon it often.

More than with the other chakras, it's very likely that your throat chakra is open in some aspects of your life, and closed off in others. Just because you possess a crippling fear of public speaking, for instance, doesn't mean you're completely mute. You might still talk with friends and family. I've had clients go the opposite way, also—they only really feel comfortable onstage, because then they can speak the truth. Put them in front of an audience of strangers and they thrive, but in a room full of friends, they withdraw into themselves.

This is another one of those chakras experiencing a shift currently. In the past, the pattern of the throat chakra has been "speak to keep the peace." It was about negotiating and focusing on the community. We're finding that ideal is changing. We're individuals, and we have our own needs. Speaking communicates our personal values, which helps the entire group in the end. A little conflict up front can prevent a big one later, and everyone will remain happier and healthier.

Speaking the truth is essential. Our throat chakra is highly connected to our root chakra—both the upper root chakra and the lower foot chakra. They provide energy to each other. When we speak truth, we see the path laid out ahead of us. This honesty keeps us on the right track. It's liberating to open your throat chakra and to speak the truth.

When you close off your throat chakra, or when you lie, you damage that path. You can't walk your true path through life if you aren't also speaking the truth. They rely upon each other. That's why silence and dishonesty are so dangerous—not only are you disconnecting from your throat chakra, but you're going to feel lost and confused in the aftermath.

Don't give power away because of fear. Nobody is going to speak up for you. Nobody knows you as well as you know yourself. You need to speak up, be honest with yourself and others, so you can live a healthy and fulfilled life.

Don't defend yourself—the truth doesn't need to be defended. Don't make excuses. Just because someone doesn't want to hear the truth, doesn't mean that it's wrong. Simply state your own truth, and people will have to deal with it. You have every right in speaking of what's best for you.

On the other hand, do not overuse your throat chakra. Drawing upon the throat chakra doesn't mean you go out and start arguments. You're not picking fights. You're not always talking. This isn't about who can talk the most. It's about speaking the truth when necessary. It's about being honest with yourself and others, so you keep your inner integrity.

Drawing on your throat chakra while speaking the truth should feel effortless. A lie is difficult. It seems easy at the time, but it only gets harder as time goes on. I lied a lot about seeing movies, for instance. A friend would ask if I'd seen such-and-such film yet. Let's use *The King's Speech* as an example. I'd say yes, because it seemed like lying was easier. I wouldn't need an explanation as to why I hadn't seen it, or throw my friend's conversation off by creating an awkward "Oh, you haven't?" moment.

In the long term, however, those lies were much harder. I couldn't go over to his house and ask to watch *The King's Speech* or come in months later wanting to talk about it. He'd be confused about why I was so excited to discuss the film again, months after he confirmed that I'd seen it. Plus, if he asked me any specific questions about the film during our initial conversation, I'd be at a loss. What was my favorite part? I can't really say "I don't know," because he thinks I've already seen it! The lie only gets more complicated if you tell two people two different stories.

Sure, whether or not I've seen a movie is a low-stakes example, but the sentiment remains. If I'd told my friend the truth, it would have been easy. I'd never have to remember what I told him, months down the line, because I would already know—I'd told him the truth. There would be no worries about conflicting stories, no worries about being caught in a lie. Simple. By lying, I've given my friend power over me. First of all, I've subsumed my own needs in favor of his. Second, I now fear how he'll react if he finds out I lied. Better not lying in the first place.

Speaking your truth and being heard feels scary. It's uncomfortable, until you get used to it. Expressing yourself, putting yourself out there for judgment, can be terrifying. That's why so many people walk around with their throat chakras closed off. In doing so, however, they're losing their way. They're losing a key aspect of their identity.

Take The FREE 3-Minute Chakra Healing Test. Find out how each of your 7 Chakras may be influencing your health and life

48   *www.VelocityHousePresents.com/chakrahealing*

The throat chakra wants to be open. That energy desires a healthy, high-vibration state. It knows when it's being unnaturally stifled. Regardless, opening the throat chakra fully is potentially one of the hardest things you'll do in life, because we're all so afraid of being judged. Because it's such a widespread issue, however, there are many solutions you can try. Techniques for reconnecting to and opening the throat chakra are nearly as numerous as the people who take advantage of them.

Do you carry a lot of tension in your jaw? One of the simplest methods for connecting to your throat chakra involves releasing that pent-up energy. This will really start the process of opening your throat chakra.

Drop your jaw as low as it will go, and rub the joint connecting your jawbone to your face. Feel all that energy stored there? Massage it out. As you do so, I'd like you to let out an "ohm" sound: a low ohm, rising up from your chest but really taking its time coming out through your throat. Let that sound open up your throat energy, even as you release the blockages from your jaw by massaging and pulling down on that joint. Repeat until your throat feels open and relaxed.

There are also tapping exercises you can use with your throat chakra. Use two fingers to tap lightly on your throat, focusing on the energy stored in your throat chakra. Repeat clearing statements as necessary until your throat chakra's energy is balanced. This will get your throat accustomed to speaking the truth and will start the healing process. For instance:

"I deserve to be heard. I enjoy speaking the truth. People want to listen to me. People want me to express myself. I can tell people what I need. I can tell people what I want. I am ready to speak up. I am letting go of the notion that I can't express myself. I am moving past my shame. I want to be heard. I am ready to be heard."

If you're feeling extra adventurous, I recommend singing the clearing statements instead of speaking them. While speaking them will certainly work, singing makes most people even more uncomfortable. The faster you accept and embrace that uncomfortable energy, the faster your throat chakra will clear out. Don't worry about singing any tune in particular. Just take a chance and sing! Find somewhere private

Take The FREE 3-Minute Chakra Healing Test. Find out how each of your 7 Chakras may be influencing your health and life

www.VelocityHousePresents.com/chakrahealing   **49**

and quiet, and really belt out your clearing statements. I promise it will make a huge difference.

Finally, you can work with visualizations to cement your connection with your throat chakra. When your throat chakra is closed off, it can feel like your vocal cords are all tangled up. You know what you want to say, and you know you should say it, but your vocal cords just won't cooperate. This can be highly frustrating, because it feels like your body is betraying you.

Focus on that image of your vocal cords tied up in knots. Imagine they're like headphones—you wrapped your headphones up nice and neat so they'd be ready when you needed them, but when you take them out of your pocket, they're tangled and thoroughly useless. You could also think of them as the extension cord you coiled up and put away, only to find it in one huge, gnarled ball when you needed it the next time.

Once you can picture your knotted vocal cords, set about untying them. Work those knots out in your mind. Open your vocal cords up and let them breathe. As you untie all those snarls, the energy in your throat chakra should follow. When you're done, you should feel your throat chakra calm down.

Oftentimes, people close their throat chakras early in life. I think it has something to do with the "children should be seen and not heard" mentality. Later on, as an adult, they can't break out of those old patterns. The energy they picked up as children is still holding them back. If this sounds familiar, you can remedy the situation with very little effort.

Whatever age you feel your throat chakra closed up, picture yourself that age. Now, talk to your younger self. Tell him or her that speaking up is okay. You know that you felt ignored as a child, but now it's time to take that power back. Hand your inner child an object symbolizing that talking is okay. I recommend a microphone. Give your inner child a voice.

Finally, there's one more exercise to reset your throat chakra. As I said earlier, your throat chakra is highly connected to your root chakra. They rely on each other for energy, and you can't follow your true path if you aren't also speaking the truth regularly. I recommend making that link between your root chakra and your throat chakra more than symbolic.

Take The FREE 3-Minute Chakra Healing Test. Find out how each of your 7 Chakras may be influencing your health and life

50   www.VelocityHousePresents.com/chakrahealing

Just as we plugged our root chakra into our foot chakra, to improve the energy flow between those two areas, we will plug our throat chakra into our root chakra. I personally envision a wire connecting my two chakras, but I've seen some people "hook" the two together, and others tie them together. Whatever method you use, picture connecting the two pools of energy. Picture them flowing into each other, the energies changing color as they pass between your root and throat chakras.

This will help you walk your true path, because your chakras will support each other. By connecting your two chakras, each becomes more open and whole. Your throat chakra will teach your root chakra how to be more honest, improving both in the long run. You will feel the energy flowing down the conduit between your root and throat chakras, and it will steer you down the right road.

This open connection is very important as we move into the last two chakras. We're entering the higher frequencies now, starting with our intuitive chakra.

CHAPTER 8

Chakra Six: Intuitive Chakra

Sixth sense. Third eye. Astral sight. Going with your gut. Reacting on instinct.

There are plenty of ways to refer to your sixth chakra, but they all boil down to one thing: intuition.[xxvii] Your intuitive chakra is located in the middle of your forehead, right in the traditional third eye region, and it's responsible for insight. Traditionally, it's associated with the color indigo, the element light, and the metal silver.[xxviii] Much like a closed foot chakra, a closed intuitive chakra will leave you feeling lost and confused. You'll feel aimless and a bit afraid.

When I was having trouble back in my twenties, a lot of it stemmed from neglecting my intuitive chakra (though I didn't know until later). I had plenty of problems with other chakras too—I'd given away too much of my power through my navel chakra, my foot chakra and root chakra weren't grounded. I was perpetually afraid of making my needs known. However, I'd wager that at least half of my resentment and anger stemmed from closing off my intuitive chakra.

I was working a dead-end job in retail, solely to pay rent. I was ambitious, but didn't know what to turn that ambition towards. I hadn't

Take The FREE 3-Minute Chakra Healing Test. Find out how each of your 7 Chakras may be influencing your health and life
www.VelocityHousePresents.com/chakrahealing

53

found my place in the world yet, and it felt like I never would. I distinctly remember waking up one morning in the winter with a headache already pounding away, bills unpaid and only a lone box of cereal to feed me for the week, feeling like nobody was there for me. I felt like life had no answers, like there was no pattern to the universe. I had no idea what I was doing, and (even worse) no idea how to fix that situation. In short, I had no purpose.

A closed off intuitive chakra is incredibly dangerous. A person without a purpose is no person at all. It doesn't matter what your purpose is or what scale it's on, you need *something* to live for. There was light all around me, but I was determined not to see it. Casting about aimlessly in the dark, I felt like the world had abandoned me. I felt neglected, and I struggled to find answers to my questions; I could not find the solutions I so desperately needed. Yet the world was trying to provide me answers the whole time. I just wasn't listening.

I was like a deaf man, or more aptly, I was like a man who willfully sealed my ears up with earplugs. Think of me, staring at a chalkboard covered in equations. After a while, I was convinced that the equations had no answer. I didn't have the skills to solve the equation, so I just kept staring at them all day in anger. I'd beat my hands against the chalkboard; I'd throw erasers, and I'd yell to the heavens, wondering why this special torture was reserved all for me.

Now imagine that the whole time, Albert Einstein was standing behind me yelling the answers into my ear. He knew the answer! He could tell me! If only I'd pulled the earplugs out of my ears, I could have spared myself so much pain and despair.

The intuitive chakra is the same. The world was trying to tell me what to do the whole time, but I had shut it out. Unfortunately, our intuitive chakra is one of the easiest to shut out. We reason the intuitive chakra out of existence. We stop listening to our instincts early in life, convinced that we're better off using logic to make decisions. We close down our intuitive chakra in favor of facts and figures. Our brain works to try to keep us safe, instead of trusting something as "unreliable" as intuition.

If your intuitive chakra is closed off, you will also feel a lot of tension in your brow area. It will feel like there's a lot of weight there, because the energy is pooling.[xxix] It's not flowing correctly. Another

Take The FREE 3-Minute Chakra Healing Test. Find out how each of your 7 Chakras may be influencing your health and life

54   *www.VelocityHousePresents.com/chakrahealing*

obvious sign of a neglected intuitive chakra is headaches. A propensity for headaches, or a pattern of bad headaches, can signify that your intuitive chakra needs attention. The world is trying to talk to you, but you're not letting it through. You're not open to its advice.

Now, the intuitive chakra is a bit more complicated than some of the others we've dealt with, because you can actually be open while still having problems. Some people are excellent at receiving intuition. They always know what their intuition is telling them. However, they don't trust their intuition. Revelations pass them by, because they were too afraid to trust their instinct.

When we rate our connection to our intuitive chakra, therefore, we rate both of these factors separately. First of all, how open is your chakra? Can you draw upon that energy reserve? Then, if the answer is yes, how much do you trust your intuition? Do you often act on its advice, or do you ignore it?

As I said, historically, the intuitive chakra is represented by the color indigo. Focus on the gleaming pool of indigo energy (or whatever color your personal chakra is represented by) in your third eye region and rate both factors—how open your intuitive chakra is, and how much you trust its revelations.

The goal is to open our intuitive chakra. It's essential for living a fulfilled, joyous life. When your intuitive chakra is open, you know your purpose. You can live your purpose. You'll feel a very strong sense of inner truth, leading you by the hand through all your endeavors. When you face challenges, you'll feel confident acting on your intuition alone.

You already hold all the answers. You know what the solution is. All that's required is you turn inwards for the solution. When you do, the answer will project itself onto the outside world. That might not sound as exciting as Albert Einstein screaming answers in your ear, but it's just as useful. Those insurmountable obstacles are nothing in comparison to the power of a fully open and trusted intuitive chakra.

The answers will come, and when they do, you'll know they're the right ones. How? There's no logical explanation. You'll just *know*. That's how intuition works. Call it instinct; call it your subconscious; call it the world providing the answers—it doesn't matter. What matters is you will have the solution at hand.

Take The FREE 3-Minute Chakra Healing Test. Find out how each of your 7 Chakras may be influencing your health and life

www.VelocityHousePresents.com/chakrahealing   **55**

Learning to listen to and trust the intuitive chakra is difficult. It requires retraining the brain into new patterns of behavior, and your brain's not going to like it. As I mentioned earlier, the brain wants to keep us alive. It sees intuition as a threat. Intuition seems unreliable, risky, fluid. The brain wants rigidity. It wants proof and responsibility, and only a very specific type of responsibility. The problem is that this primitive part of our brain goes too far. It severs our entire connection from the intuitive chakra, even when it is not a matter of life and death. It's like locking someone in jail when all they really needed was a speeding ticket.

To use our intuitive chakra, then, we must shut down our brain. Quiet your rational, doubting side of the brain and learn to listen. Trust comes later; first we must hear what the intuitive chakra is trying to say.

Silence that primitive, survival-oriented part of the brain by redirecting blood elsewhere. Press on your neurovascular points, to draw blood into the higher regions of the brain. If I'm alone and can get away with it, I often like to press my forehead flat on the ground. First of all, it's a very comforting position, with the world supporting your mind. Second, it's a most effective method to draw blood away from your primitive brain and into your higher faculties. Once you've done that, just sit and think about whatever problems you face. Be ready to listen when the answer comes to you.

Another method I use to quiet my mind requires a standard deck of cards. I like talking aloud about my problems while flipping over the cards one at a time. Flipping the cards gives my mind something to focus on so it doesn't interfere with my intuitive chakra. Normally, I have a clear idea of what to do after running through the deck a few times.

This is the same principle behind thinking about your problems in the shower—your brain is just distracted enough to get out of the way of your intuitive chakra, allowing you to recognize insights you might miss otherwise. That's why so many great ideas seem to arise in the shower. Your brain is uncluttered, leaving your intuitive chakra ready to receive these thoughts.

Other similar places to think about your problems include long drives on an empty highway, mowing the lawn and taking a long walk.

Take The FREE 3-Minute Chakra Healing Test. Find out how each of your 7 Chakras may be influencing your health and life

56   www.VelocityHousePresents.com/chakrahealing

In each case, your conscious mind is occupied by the current task, but your brain doesn't require all faculties to process what is basically repetitive information. This leaves your intuitive chakra free to ponder your problems and come up with solutions. It's a fantastic system, provided you can take advantage of it.

I find it very helpful to ask the right questions, while touching my intuitive chakra. Sometimes it's hard to decipher what our intuition is telling us. If we leave ourselves too many options, it's difficult to determine which one we should choose. What I like to do, then, is rephrase the question. Perhaps I'll narrow down my options, and then I'll go through them one by one and ask myself if each is the right answer.

"Is this correct?" I'll ask, and then my intuitive chakra will come through. It will tell me yes or no, and I'll instinctively know whether to go with that solution or cast it aside. I like asking myself the question aloud, because it triggers my intuitive chakra. It lets the energy know "this is something we need to pay attention to. This is important."

If I'm having an important conversation with someone, I'll try to phrase my questions so they trigger the person's intuition also. "Is that correct?" is useful, because people already *know* the answer, whether or not they admit it consciously. As soon as you ask that question, they know what the right answer is.

Then there are the more traditional methods for getting in touch with the third eye, which involve visualization. Still, this isn't visualization the way it was once handled. We used to think a lot of effort had to be expended in order to open our intuitive chakra. You really had to sit and focus in order to get the most benefit.

Nowadays, we know that's simply not true. We can use visualization without sacrificing our time and energies. A lot of low-effort visualization can be just as useful as a little high-effort visualization. Your intuitive chakra shows you the correct path. Traditionally, we think of the third eye like a window. It's as if our insight enters through a portal.

Reverse that. Your third eye is lighting your way. It's showing you the path. Picture your third eye like a big spotlight coming out of your forehead, or like a headlamp that miners use. When you're out for a walk, imagine that indigo light shining out of your forehead and onto the ground in front of you. It's illuminating your path. It tells you that you're going in the right direction. It knows the way, even if you don't. When you do this, you open your intuitive chakra further and learn to trust its insight.

Dream journals are also helpful. When you wake up in the middle of the night and feel like some insight is right on the edge of your brain, grab that journal and a pen and start writing down whatever you can remember. The more you chronicle your dreams, the better you'll get at recalling them. Your brain *wants* you to recall the insight you discovered in your dreams; that's why it woke you up in the first place. Learn to remember those insights in order to take advantage of them.

Of course, you can also do more intense (some might say tradition-al) meditations to open your intuitive chakra. That's completely fine also. These days I'm very in-tune with my intuitive chakra, and I tend to meditate on my third eye quite a bit. Whenever I have a quiet moment, I'll take the time and focus on my intuitive chakra. It's calming; it's simple once you get the hang of it, and it keeps the conduit open so I can draw upon that energy whenever I need it.

Regardless of the method you choose, you'll get better at contacting your intuitive chakra the more you do it. When your intuitive chakra is closed off or neglected, your insights are scarce. They'll randomly enter your mind now and then, but it's haphazard.

The more you consult your intuitive chakra, the less sporadic those insights will seem. You'll habitually consult your third eye for answers, and it will be rarer that you find no answer. Once you get past the initial hurdles, it's easy to maintain an open and connected intuitive chakra.

As your intuitive chakra fills and opens, you must also connect with your other chakras. All three of your lower chakras require energy from your sixth chakra in order to reach higher vibration levels. Just like we did with the root and foot chakras, or the root and throat chakras, we need to connect the intuitive chakra with others.

As I said in the last chapter, concerning the throat and root chakras, there are numerous ways you can forge a connection. The method you choose is a matter of personal preference. I normally envision "wires" between my chakras. I run circuits for the energy transfers, as if my body contained power cables.

Take The FREE 3-Minute Chakra Healing Test. Find out how each of your 7 Chakras may be influencing your health and life

58   www.VelocityHousePresents.com/chakrahealing

I've seen people use numerous other methods, however. Some people elect to "hook" their chakras together with their hands, for instance. They'll make a hook from the index fingers on both hands, placing the hooks on each of the two chakras they want to join. Then they'll pull the two hooks together, as if dragging part of the chakras along, and couple the two. Whatever you use is fine, as long as the result is a free and open energy flow between the two chakras in question.

So join your intuitive chakra to each of the three lower chakras: the root, the sacral, and the navel. Ensure that your connections are sound and flowing correctly before moving onto the final chakra: the crown.

CHAPTER 9

Chakra Seven: The Crown Chakra

We've now reached the last of the eight chakras we experience in the physical realm. We've also come full-circle in terms of purpose. We started this book with the foot chakra, which keeps us grounded and connected to the energy reserves of Earth. The crown chakra complements the foot chakra.

Our crown chakra also keeps us "grounded," but not to Earth. Instead, our crown chakra connects us to the sky, to our spirituality and the upper chakras that constitute the higher realm.[xxx]

The crown chakra and the intuitive chakra are close partners. Both involve opening our minds and listening. However, the sources of inspiration are different. While the intuitive chakra requires self-reflection and a willingness to turn inward, the crown chakra demands that we look outwards—that we connect to the world at large and whatever constitutes the higher power you believe in.

I said in the last chapter that I had a lot of problems with my intuitive chakra during my twenties. I felt lost, like I never had the answers. I wandered aimlessly, hoping to find guidance. While my inner self was silent, my outer self was also.

One of the first steps I took was to turn to religion. I was never exceedingly religious as a child. We celebrated Christmas, but I knew more about Santa than I did about Jesus. I never really knew what Easter was all about until I was a teenager, and we probably went to church once or twice a year at most. Still, I thought religion was worth a try as a confused young adult. It seemed to have answers, and many people took solace in faith. It was worth a try.

"I hope you find what you're looking for," the pastor said to me, when I explained why I was joining his congregation. He was a great listener and still is a good friend of mine, but he didn't know how to help. All he could do was send love in my direction and pray that I found the guidance I needed.

Nothing. I felt nothing. I knelt down and prayed; I went to church every Sunday; I tried living a good and kind life, and still I felt nothing. I had no answers to my prayers, no responses from this God I'd put my trust in. I went to a very negative place. How could all these people take solace from something that did *nothing* for me? Were they naïve? What was the secret? I prayed so hard for guidance and got silence in return.

I felt angry at God. I'd wager that you know what I mean, if you've ever been in the same position. I *hated* God. On the cross, Jesus shouted, "Father, why hast thou forsaken me?" In my anger and confusion, I felt the same way. I felt like I must be unworthy in some way, like I didn't deserve help from the spiritual realm. I felt betrayed. Little did I know that the problem was mine all along.

I want you to take a moment and visualize your crown chakra. Traditionally we associate this chakra with the color purple, the element thought and the metal gold, but your personal chakra might differ.[xxxi] Regardless, the name is very apt: the crown chakra sits at the top of your head, just like a crown would. However, the crown chakra is special when compared to other chakras. It's not just a pool of energy residing somewhere in your body. Think of it like a large window. A portal into your mind might be a better description. The crown chakra is a doorway. Just like a window, your crown chakra has two states: open and shut.

My crown chakra was closed off. At some point in my childhood, I closed the window over my crown chakra. Not only had I closed it

Take The FREE 3-Minute Chakra Healing Test. Find out how each of your 7 Chakras may be influencing your health and life

62

www.VelocityHousePresents.com/chakrahealing

off—I *sealed* it off. I'd closed the window, then nailed the window frame down and caulked the whole thing shut. I prayed and prayed, but I wasn't open to any guidance. I felt betrayed by the silence, but I caused the issue to begin with.

It took a long time to open my crown—longer than any of the other chakras. I was too bitter, too jaded. I read the texts; I knew all the benefits, but I found it hard to trust. The intuitive chakra I understood. I knew how to rely on myself. I just found it hard relying on an outside force.

Yet, slowly but surely, my anger died out. As I opened my heart chakra and learned forgiveness, as I learned to walk a true path, and to speak the truth, as I claimed back my power and became comfortable with myself—and, frankly, as I grew older and the fire started to die out—I felt something start to give. I started feeling lonelier, more disconnected than ever. My life was better than ever, but something was missing. I knew that something related to my still-closed crown chakra.

When we cut ourselves off from the spiritual realm, we still pine for it. We long the welcoming of that fold. The longer I waited, the more egregious my shuttered crown chakra became.

An open crown chakra is an incredible gift. The crown chakra connects us to the spiritual realm, which means more than you might think. A person with an open crown chakra is more charitable, for instance, and finds more wonder in the world.

More importantly, however, an open crown chakra means an end to loneliness. It means an end to feeling cut off or unworthy. When we open our crown chakra, we allow ourselves to be one with divinity. We dispel the illusion of a separation from "God," for lack of a better term. We feel oneness with that higher realm. It ends that longing for divinity, by granting us divinity.

I opened my crown chakra, and the world opened with it. I felt connected to something much greater than myself. I felt watched over, cared for by some unseen presence. I finally understood where I fit in the world. All of my other chakras, which I thought were open prior to connecting with my crown chakra, expanded even further. I hadn't known how much I wasn't experiencing by keeping a tight lid on my crown chakra. Once I did know, it was impossible to go back.

I'm still not a very religious person, per se. I don't go to church very often, and I sometimes forget about Lent. On the other hand, I'm intensely spiritual. I keep my crown chakra as open as I can handle at all times, reveling in that feeling of oneness. In my twenties, I feared I'd never experience that sense of belonging. I wish I could go back and tell my younger self what he was doing wrong. It would have saved us both a bunch of trouble.

I can hear my crown chakra speak to me. "I am one with God, whose energy and love flows through me and keeps me on my true path." The conception of God as something separate and above us is misguided and outdated. Cast it off. When we open our crown chakra, we become a piece of God.

Please note: I still use the term God because of the way I was raised, but you're welcome to substitute your own belief system in that spot. The important part is not the terminology, but the result.

When your crown chakra is open, you'll feel that energy constantly rushing through you. It is energy at a very high vibrational level, and you will feel it bolstering your other chakras in turn. They will rise to new levels by the addition of the crown chakra's energies.

In fact, one of the first things I recommend you do after opening your crown chakra is plugging it into your foot chakra. Connect the two, just like we've done previously with other pairings. Visualize the wire running out of your crown chakra and into the base of your foot chakra, the energy flowing unimpeded.

It's very important that we connect the crown and foot chakras because they need to work together. The crown chakra helps keep the foot chakra on the right path, and the foot chakra helps us not become overwhelmed by the energy in the crown chakra. We love these higher frequency energies that get drawn in through the crown chakra, but they're exhausting. When we connect to our foot chakra, we draw that energy out into the world and help our bodies use the energy from the spiritual realm instead of being distracted by it.

This will also help if you start having headaches related to your crown chakra. The crown chakra is funny, in that when it's closed, we have headaches and migraines, but when it's open we can also experience occasional headaches. The higher vibrations of the energy bombarding

Take The FREE 3-Minute Chakra Healing Test. Find out how each of your 7 Chakras may be influencing your health and life

64

www.VelocityHousePresents.com/chakrahealing

your open crown chakra can wreak havoc on your brain.[xxxii] It's great to be open to the spiritual realm, but it takes some getting used to. Plugging our crown chakra into our foot chakra can help alleviate these headaches as we become accustomed to our oneness with God.

This is also the only chakra that I recommend opening gradually, for your own safety. Connecting to the spirit realm can be scary and overwhelming. Take it a little bit at a time, and the process will go smoother. There's less risk involved. I've known people who opened their crown chakra too fast and really weren't ready for the energy involved. Better to take it slow and safe, building up your tolerance a bit at a time.

On that note, let's take a moment here to rate your crown chakra connection. How open does it feel on the standard zero-to-ten scale? Do you feel lost and alone, or do you already feel like you're one with the divine? Can you feel the high-vibration energies of the spiritual realm coursing through you?

Additionally, let's rate your tolerance. I've worked with many clients who, upon opening their crown chakras, became very upset and angry with the world. They started looking at the state of the world, at wars and hatred and these products of our lower-vibration selves, and they became infuriated. How could these things happen?

The problem is not ours to question. Sure, we create these terrible things, but they are our creations and we must learn acceptance. We must learn to accept they have a purpose, even thought if may be obscured. You don't need to love these aspects of our nature, but you must try to forgive them. Forgive and move on. You need to release your anger, and sever your energetic connection with these unwanted aspects before they wound your crown chakra. Anger is a distortion of the knowledge that the crown chakra gives you. Forgiveness is the ultimate goal.

You will feel these lower-frequency energies, and you will want to rebel against them. Don't. They will stop you anyway, and you'll fight a pointless battle. Accept these lower frequencies. Let them become a part of you. Over the course of time, you'll become immune to them.

Instead of trying to change your energy patterns, make new ones. Bring in your higher vibrations and make new patterns from them.

Take The FREE 3-Minute Chakra Healing Test. Find out how each of your 7 Chakras may be influencing your health and life
www.VelocityHousePresents.com/chakrahealing

65

Once they're built and solid, build a bridge between the two patterns. Let the higher energies raise up the lower ones. This is how you'll learn acceptance instead of anger.

So once you've rated the openness of your crown chakra, rate how much anger you feel versus how much forgiveness. A zero means that you're caught on these horrible happenings in the world, and you can't see any purpose for them. You're very angry. A ten means that you have accepted that these lower vibration creations still have a purpose and a place in the world. I'm not going to lie, a ten is incredibly hard to achieve. Don't be shocked if you fall somewhere on the lower end of the spectrum—it's human nature. If you do, at least you know where you can improve.

As I said earlier, opening your crown chakra can be very difficult. I will provide you with a number of techniques, but don't be surprised if you run through a bunch of them and don't feel anything happening. Hopefully, however, one of the methods I'm including in this chapter will help.

The first three use your body to enhance your connection: headstands, head rolls and fasting. Headstands and head rolls concentrate your energies around your crown chakra. When you do a headstand, you are pressing your crown chakra against the ground and uniting those two energy reserves. This can be a very welcome feeling, and an easy technique to practice. Head rolls draw energy into your head and exploit the physical motion in order to enhance your connection to the crown chakra.

Fasting works a bit differently. Fasting is effective, because we deny our physical needs to enhance our spirituality. Similar to silencing our primitive mind while working with our intuitive chakra, fasting helps us turn off our physical needs. We give up our need for food to attain a higher spiritual connection.

Along those lines, you can use meditation and prayer to open your crown chakra. It's not going to work for everyone—I used to go to church, pray and then get frustrated when there was no response—but it can help. When we meditate or pray, we create higher vibration energies. We start to align our bodies to take advantage of those higher energies, and we naturally begin to draw them in through our crown

Take The FREE 3-Minute Chakra Healing Test. Find out how each of your 7 Chakras may be influencing your health and life

66   *www.VelocityHousePresents.com/chakrahealing*

chakra. For the best results, I recommend making time to meditate or pray daily. Don't let it become routine or rote, because you'll find you're tuning out instead of actually focusing, but make time to sit and connect with your crown chakra each day.

Maybe you believe in God, and you're ready to open your crown chakra, but you've yet to experience oneness with the divinity. You have a very clear idea of "God" and "self," and never the two shall meet. What I want you to do is unbox God. Remove the walls that you've placed around God in your mind.

Now you might say, "I did that, and now there's nothing there." That's true. There's nothing in the box, and you can't *see* God anymore. Before, you could look at that box and say "There's God." Now you can't see the spiritual realm, and it's scary. It feels like there's nothing there at all.

Relax. God is still there. In fact, God is everywhere. You are a part of God, as is everything. When you box God up, you reduce the power of the spiritual realm. You're saying that God is only allowed in certain parts of your life. Let God go, and then trust that you're not alone. You're still being watched over. Let God out of the cell you've built.

Finally, we can improve our connection to the crown chakra with affirmations. This can help cement your connection with divinity and improve your sense of oneness. Place a hand on your crown chakra (the top of your head), focus on that purple window into your spirit, and begin affirming your link with the higher realm.

"I am connected with the spiritual realm. I am receiving inspiration. I am receiving guidance. I deserve to know truth. I am true to myself. I am experiencing God. I hold God within me, as a part of me. I am connected with a higher purpose. I am not lost anymore. I know what to do. I know where to go. I am ready to face all obstacles in my path, with God beside me."

As always, feel free to replace "God" with any higher being you prefer. Be strong in your assertions. Be firm. As you recite these affirmations, you should feel your sense of oneness, of connection, growing more powerful. I like to begin each day with this exercise. It keeps my crown chakra open and prepares my body for receiving those higher frequency energies.

Finally, we should make one more connection. We've already connected our crown chakra to our foot chakra, but there's more we can do. Specifically, I'd recommend connecting your crown chakra with your navel chakra. Visualize wires or hooks or whatever you'd like, but make sure those two are connected. This way, you connect your spiritual nature to your unique and grounded personality. The soul is helping guide the self along its path.

The soul guiding the self—what a powerful image to end this chapter. Open your crown chakra, allow spirituality into your life in all its forms, become one with divinity, and you will know your purpose. It's like your soul, radiant with light, reached out, took a hold of your hand and showed you the way. Whether you're Christian or not, I've always found the words, "I was blind, but now I see," very representative of the moment when you first open your crown chakra. It's as if a veil has been pulled back from the world, and you're seeing everything for the first time. I don't even have the words to describe it.

It's something you're just going to have to experience for yourself.

Exercises

Now that you've read through the book once, I want to give you the best experience as you move forward and improve your chakras. A large part of that process entails making it as easy as possible for you to go back and work on any chakra you feel is closed off. For your convenience, therefore, I've gone back through the book and compiled the exercises from every chapter into this one section. You can flip directly to the exercises pertaining to the chakra you want to work on. Keep it around as a resource that you turn to in the spare moments of your day, when you have a quiet moment to connect with your chakras.

I'm trying to make this as easy as possible for you, the reader. I know that I, personally, would have appreciated a resource like this when I was starting out. I hope it will be a big help as you continue to work on your energy.

Take The FREE 3-Minute Chakra Healing Test. Find out how each of your 7 Chakras may be influencing your health and life

68   www.VelocityHousePresents.com/chakrahealing

Chakra Zero – Foot Chakra

Look at your feet: Our eyes are great at directing energy. We focus our efforts on whatever we're looking at. Concentrate on your feet, so that they'll eventually show you the way. Go on long walks every day, just staring at your feet the whole time. Leave the house looking down at your feet and get back home still looking at your feet, all without looking up a single time. This will direct energy at your feet and help ground your foot chakra. Walking around town or just walking around the house, look down at your feet and throw some energy down there.

Sometimes when using this technique, I even recommend making it more visual. Try picturing the energy as it flows to your feet. Imagine how your feet would look when receiving that energy. It's like a warm beam of light shining out of your eyes and falling on your glowing feet. Use that visualization while walking, to stimulate your foot chakra.

Stretch out your arm and trace a circle on the ground around you. This is the typical boundary of your foot chakra. Once you can clearly see the outline of your own foot chakra, push it outward. Expand the boundary. Let it grow and encompass more of the ground you stand on. Imagine that this entire area is filled with energy, like red-hot lava or beams of light rising up from the Earth. Focus on drawing that energy into your body. Picture it swirling toward you, entering your body through your feet. Before long, you should feel a warmth in your feet and a growing sense of purpose. This signifies the connection to your foot chakra growing stronger. You should see your path laid out in front of you. Literally, you should be able to picture a glowing cord, starting at your feet and stretching far into the distance, keeping your life on course.

Picture your foot chakra's damaged or blocked energy field in your mind. It's a chaotic mass of light and darkness, fighting for control. There will be lots of swirling energies, lots of disruptions. There will be none of the safety and security that we usually hope for in our energy reserves. This energy will feel foreign and make you feel uneasy, but you must immerse yourself in it before things can get better. Embrace the idea of failure. Don't let it scare you. Let the uncomfortable, damaged energy wrap around you. It will make you sick. If you're really connected to your foot chakra, you might even feel the soles of your feet tingling. Get rid of that energy. Clear that sickening, failure-prone energy right out of the space. Use your feet, physically taking over the space. Kick your feet firmly outwards, flinging the energy out of the soles of your feet. Claim the space as your own.

If you want, feel free to state some affirmations out loud: "I'm releasing the fear that I'm going to lose everything," or "I'm releasing my fear of failure."

Chakra One – Root Chakra

Color:	**Red**
Element:	**Earth**
Metal:	**Lead**
Animal:	**Snake**

Focus on your root chakra. Picture a red-hot ball of energy around your groin and tailbone. It will be like molten lead, cradled in your hips. Probe that energy with your mind. Hold your hand over this area of your body and feel the warmth radiating from your chakra. Hopefully you'll feel a strong connection to this energy reservoir, but if you don't, it's likely that your root chakra is unbalanced in some way. Problems may manifest in one of three categories: money, health and relationships.

MONEY

Try carrying money around in your pocket every day—not just a credit or a debit card, but real cash. Feel the energy that money has. There's a reason they say money will "burn a hole in your pocket." There's a real energy you feel when you have cash money at hand. You can feel the money's presence. Bring some cash with you the next time you go out, and see if you feel more connected to your root chakra at the end of the day.

HEALTH

When you are constantly weighing yourself, you're bringing negative energy into your body. You're throwing off your body's natural rhythm and trying to force it into a new shape. You're not persuading your

Take The FREE 3-Minute Chakra Healing Test. Find out how each of your 7 Chakras may be influencing your health and life

70   *www.VelocityHousePresents.com/chakrahealing*

body—you're punishing your body. Stop! Let your body work itself out. Accept your body. Give it permission to change, but don't force it into any particular shape. Stop obsessively weighing yourself, and things will hopefully get better!

RELATIONSHIPS

You must allow your relationships to thrive; the only way of doing so is through self-acceptance and self-love. Don't be what others want you to be. Be yourself.

A lot of relationship problems stem from birth energy. Few births are perfect, and thus we're left with this imperfect energy after delivery. Visualize the perfect birth, and shape your birth energy into an ideal form. Imagine your mother carried you until you were ready to be born and that the delivery itself was smooth and quick. Imagine the love and acceptance from your parents and relatives after your birth. This will get you back on the right time line and reset your birth energy to a healthier state.

Again, I feel it's important to mention that your root chakra could be suffering from any combination of money, health, and relationship issues. They're not mutually exclusive in any way.

Imagine that your spinal cord doesn't end around your tailbone. Imagine that it, in fact, hangs out of your tailbone, like a wire. Take that wire and plug it into your foot chakra. Feel the live current rushing from the foot chakra into your root chakra. Can you feel all that energy you now have access to? Put it to use in your dealings with money, in your pursuit of good health, in your relationships. Let them thrive. Your foot chakra isn't a great outlet. It's one of those old, loose outlets where the plug occasionally slips out of the wall. You might go days without any problems, only for the plug to slip out randomly. When it does, just plug it back in. Keep that energy flowing.

Now we will clear out the old energy from your root chakra. Picture your root chakra as a molten ball of lead, right in your groin area, in the center of your hips. Focus on that red-hot energy, the snake coiled around it, and try to hold that image in your mind. Once the image is stable, go into your root chakra, and see where you're wounded. Maybe it's bad birth energy or just an unbalanced area. Maybe you can picture

Take The FREE 3-Minute Chakra Healing Test. Find out how each of your 7 Chakras may be influencing your health and life

www.VelocityHousePresents.com/chakrahealing

71

the wounds that are causing your relationships strife or that are causing you to hold on to this extra weight. These wounds will look like dark blotches on the surface of your beautiful, red energy. Just like with our foot chakra, this blotchy energy will feel uncomfortable. It's *supposed* to feel uncomfortable. That's how we know we're in the right spot.

Now dump that bad energy. Scoop it out by the handful and dump it on the ground. Get rid of it. Let it be absorbed back into the Earth from whence it came. As you do so, I recommend stating to yourself what the problem is. For example:

"I'm releasing this energy. I can never hold on to my money. I am bad at handling my finances. I spend money needlessly. I waste money. I am foolish with cash. I can't be responsible. I will not amount to anything if I keep up these habits."

Take all that, and get rid of it. Throw it out. Now think of that beautiful red energy again, of the snake and the lead and the earth that embody your root chakra. Use those to fill the empty space you created. You don't want to leave your root chakra with no energy. You don't want to leave it barren. That allows all sorts of chaos to enter the space. Instead, fill your root chakra with the new energy. Fill it with the correct color. Turn it into a haven for your snake or whatever personalized animal lives in your root chakra. Make it into a safe place, aligned with your body's needs. Heal those wounds by replacing the tainted energy with the correct energy.

Chakra Two – Sacral Chakra

Color: **Orange**
Element: **Fire**
Metal: **Tin**
Animal: **Jaguar**

The sacral chakra is located in the middle of your stomach (and the corresponding spot on your back), approximately two or three finger-widths above the root chakra. I've always thought of the sacral chakra as a warm fireplace full of energy in my stomach. Now focus on your sacral chakra. Focus on that orange fireplace in your abdomen, a jaguar curled up next to it.

Take The FREE 3-Minute Chakra Healing Test. Find out how each of your 7 Chakras may be influencing your health and life

72   *www.VelocityHousePresents.com/chakrahealing*

The best part about the sacral chakra is that reconnecting and healing its energy is so much fun. In fact, the sacral chakra is my favorite to work on, because it simply requires pampering your primal, lustful side. Some examples I've used in the past to help people: long warm showers, highly self-indulgent meals (lots of steak and chocolate), walks by the beach, candlelight, massages and tantric sex.

When I feel like I'm growing a bit distant from my sacral chakra, I like to start my day by welcoming pleasure: something along the lines of "Today, something will happen that I find pleasurable and take joy from." This simple statement sets the Law of Attraction at work.

If you're dealing with old wounds in your sacral chakra, however, you should clear out the old energy before you can fully heal. Using your flattened hand, begin tapping on your stomach at a steady pace, right where your sacral chakra is located. This will help you focus on your sacral chakra and being stirring the energy kept within. From there, start repeating clearing statements. Speak the thoughts that you're trying to purge from your energy center. For instance, you could start with:

"I'm going to clear this old energy. I'm allowing my sacral chakra to clean itself. I'm letting go of these negative feelings. I'm letting go of this anger and this frustration. I'm allowing myself to feel pleasure. I'm allowing myself to love sex. I'm letting go of what's holding me back. I am ready to heal. I embrace sexuality and pleasure."

Just say whatever is honestly on your mind or whatever you feel is holding you back. Be specific. Tell your chakra what to clear out. I also find that blinking helps with the clearing process; scientists think blinking helps us refocus our thoughts. Blink rhythmically while you say the clearing statements and help your brain reset your neural pathways into these new, healthier patterns.

Once you've done that, picture the fireplace in your stomach once again. Can you see where the bad energy is? Can you see where it's unhealthy? Maybe it's places where your fireplace isn't burning quite as brightly or has gone out entirely. Scoop that old energy out, like it is ashes and charred logs. Put it back into the ground, where it belongs. Of course, that might not clear it all out. Now concentrate on your sacral chakra.

Take The FREE 3-Minute Chakra Healing Test. Find out how each of your 7 Chakras may be influencing your health and life

www.VelocityHousePresents.com/chakrahealing　　　　**73**

The sacral chakra is like a little furnace. Turn your furnace on and burn away any remnants of that bad energy. Heat your sacral chakra up so it burns away that old, wounded energy. Then take a deep breath, filling your sacral chakra back up with clean, pure energy. Repeat as many times as necessary until your sacral chakra is clear and open.

Sexual abuse as a child also affects the sacral chakra, and has its own associated technique for clearing. In my experience, the most effective method is communicating with your inner child. Grab a journal and write to your inner child. Say hello. Say that you understand what happened back then was not okay. Then, switch hands. Put your pen in your non-dominant hand, where your handwriting is probably worse—it will look more like a kid's handwriting. Let your inner child write. Let him or her talk about emotions and anger and frustrations. Let him or her take over and communicate with you. Give your inner child a voice. This process—letting your younger self write out its problems—is allowing your inner child to take advantage of clearing statements. That younger version of you is literally helping your sacral chakra know what needs cleared by expressing its emotions.

Chakra Three – Navel Chakra

Color:	**Yellow**
Element:	**Water**
Metal:	**Iron**
Animal:	**Hummingbird**

Think of your navel chakra, located in your upper abdomen, like a river. Picture the Mississippi or Colorado River. A river is powerful. It's just water, but it's immensely powerful. The water doesn't try to control its surroundings. The surroundings get out of the way of the river. The river's course seems natural. Sometimes the river is calm and quiet, sometimes the river is thrashing, but regardless the river follows its course.

Grab a pen and paper, if you'd like, and list off all the things you associate with power. Some common ones I hear from clients are money, sex, control, bossing people around, and knowledge. Recognize that

Take The FREE 3-Minute Chakra Healing Test. Find out how each of your 7 Chakras may be influencing your health and life

74

www.VelocityHousePresents.com/chakrahealing

these are just surrogates for power, and not true power. When you associate these things with power, you allow them to have power over you.

We're going to get in touch with our primal side. Be a warrior. Go into a safe place and yell. Give out a huge war cry. Get excited. Break out of your patterns. Break some plates against a wall. Do something crazy that embraces that primitive side and gets your adrenaline pumping. Get in touch with this power inside of you.

It doesn't need to be a huge act. Try simply changing your routine every day. We like routines, because we like controlling our day. Don't let yourself fall into patterns of behavior anymore; introduce something new so that your energy is constantly shifting.

Going for a hike always makes me feel powerful—connecting to nature while simultaneously conquering my body.

Another exercise: I want you to tap on what we call the "Karate Chop Point." That's the fleshy side of your hand, the part that you would use if you were going to chop a board in half. Use two fingers of one hand to tap on the Karate Chop Point of the other (doesn't matter which hand plays each role). As we tap, we will use something called setup statements to purge our old energy:

"Even though I give my power away too often, I'm ready to change that. Even though I've given my power to others, I am ready to reclaim it. Even though I have been controlling in the past, I am ready to improve. Even though I have tried so hard to please others, I'm ready to look after my own needs for once."

Try writing some of your own statements that are more specific to your own situation. Remember, it's an acknowledgment of the problem, followed by an acceptance of the problem and a willingness to move past it. As you work, you should feel the energies stirring. Once you've identified the breadth of the problem, reach in and remove those bad energies. Release them back into the ground, and fill your navel chakra with new, clean energy. Immediately after you clear out the old energy, do some of those aggressive exercises we discussed earlier. Break some plates or do some primal screaming. Let that new, pure energy rush in and fill the void we just left.

Take The FREE 3-Minute Chakra Healing Test. Find out how each of your 7 Chakras may be influencing your health and life

www.VelocityHousePresents.com/chakrahealing　　　　　　**75**

Chakra Four – Heart Chakra

Color:	**Green**
Element:	**Air**
Metal:	**Copper**
Animal:	**Eagle**

Concentrate on your heart chakra. Put your hand over your heart, right above that energy center. It's almost as if you were saying the Pledge of Allegiance. Stay focused and repeat the words: "I'm okay, no matter what happens." You can change it up, if you'd like. Change the wording as you go, narrowing your focus. "I feel loved, no matter what happens," or "I have all the love I need and that comforts me." Anything that plays on the theme that you are loved and the love you receive arises internally. Repeat it as long as you feel is necessary. This repetition technique is excellent for settling your heart chakra. If you've recently taken a light wound to your heart chakra or feel like it's restless, repeating, "I'm okay no matter what happens," can help calm down the energy and realign it into healthy patterns.

Another great technique I take advantage of regularly is the "It feels scary because..." pattern. When you close off your heart chakra, it might feel like you've walled it up. You've built this fortress around your heart to keep it safe. An open heart chakra recognizes that these walls are unnecessary and, in fact, harmful. We use the "It feels scary because..." method to get in touch with our feelings. Place your hand on your heart again, and finish the sentence:

"*It feels scary because someone could hurt me. It feels scary because I'm afraid to open up. It feels scary because I don't like commitments. It feels scary because people might not love me as much as I love them.*"

Comfort your scared self. Tell yourself it's safe—that you don't need to rely on anyone else for love. Accept yourself. Visualization is also a great complement to this technique. Just as we've done with the other chakras, I want you to picture the energy in your heart chakra. Imagine your heart as a glowing ball of light, too bright for others to even look at. It's like you have a miniature sun in your chest. Once you have a clear vision of your heart chakra, straining with light, begin

Take The FREE 3-Minute Chakra Healing Test. Find out how each of your 7 Chakras may be influencing your health and life

76   *www.VelocityHousePresents.com/chakrahealing*

tapping on your chest with the palm of your hand. As you do so, being releasing your fears:

"I am clearing this old energy from my heart chakra. I am ready to love myself. I am ready to give others my love. I'm not afraid that others will hurt me, because I believe in myself. I refuse to be heartbroken. My heart is open and ready to receive this energy. I am ready to commit. I am ready to love and be loved."

Clear that old energy out of your heart chakra. Watch it flow out of you and back into the ground. Then push more energy into your heart chakra. If there are walls around your heart chakra, you'll see them start to bulge outward. You'll see your heart chakra straining against those bonds, the eagle desperately seeking freedom. Keep filling your heart chakra with more energy until those walls can't take it anymore. Watch the walls explode, your heart chakra shining out in all its glory, and the eagle bursting from its cage. Notice that it doesn't feel hurt. It feels safe. It feels warm. It feels joyous.

Then, wall it back up. That's right, build those walls around your heart again. Close it off. Notice how dim everything feels. Notice how stunted your emotions feel. Start filling your heart back up with energy. Push it up against the walls of that box one more time until the box blows open again. Look inside the box at your heart, and see that it's okay. It's undamaged. Repeat this as many times as you'd like, until you're satisfied that your heart can't be hurt. It can't be damaged, unless you let it.

Chakra Five – Throat Chakra

Color: **Sapphire Blue**
Element: **Ether**
Metal: **Mercury**

Take a moment and envision a reservoir of sapphire blue energy liquid mercury nestled in the hollow of your throat. This is your throat chakra. Do you carry a lot of tension in your jaw? One of the simplest methods for connecting to your throat chakra involves releasing that pent-up energy. This will really start the process of opening your throat chakra.

Take The FREE 3-Minute Chakra Healing Test. Find out how each of your 7 Chakras may be influencing your health and life

www.VelocityHousePresents.com/chakrahealing   **77**

Drop your jaw as low as it will go, and rub the joint connecting your jawbone to your face. Feel all that energy stored there? Massage it out. As you do so, let out an "ohm" sound. Let that "ohm" open up your throat energy, even as you release the blockages from your jaw by massaging and pulling down on that joint. Repeat until your throat feels open and relaxed.

There are also tapping exercises you can use with your throat chakra. Use two fingers to tap lightly on your throat, focusing on the energy stored in your throat chakra. Repeat clearing statements as necessary until your throat chakra's energy is balanced. This will get your throat accustomed to speaking the truth and will start the healing process. For instance:

"I deserve to be heard. I enjoy speaking the truth. People want to listen to me. People want me to express myself. I can tell people what I need. I can tell people what I want. I am ready to speak up. I am letting go of the notion that I can't express myself. I am moving past my shame. I want to be heard. I am ready to be heard."

If you're feeling extra adventurous, I recommend singing the clearing statements instead of speaking them. While speaking them will certainly work, singing makes most people even more uncomfortable. The faster you accept and embrace that uncomfortable energy, the faster your throat chakra will clear out.

You can also work with visualizations to cement your connection with your throat chakra. When your throat chakra is closed off, it can feel like your vocal cords are all tangled up. Focus on the image of your vocal cords tied up in knots. Once you can picture your knotted vocal cords, set about untying them. Work those knots out in your mind. Open your vocal cords up and let them breathe. As you untie all those snarls, the energy in your throat chakra should follow. When you're done, you should feel your throat chakra calm down.

Often, people close their throat chakras early on in life. Later on, as an adult, they can't break out of those old patterns. The energy they picked up as children is still holding them back. Whatever age you feel your throat chakra closed up, picture yourself that age. Now, talk to your younger self. Tell him or her that speaking up is okay. You know that you felt ignored as a child, but now it's time to take that power

Take The FREE 3-Minute Chakra Healing Test. Find out how each of your 7 Chakras may be influencing your health and life

78   *www.VelocityHousePresents.com/chakrahealing*

back. Hand your inner child an object symbolizing it's okay to talk. I recommend a microphone. Give your inner child a voice.

There's one more exercise we can do to reset your throat chakra. Your throat chakra is highly connected to your root chakra. They rely on each other for energy, and you can't follow your true path if you aren't also speaking the truth regularly. I recommend making that link between your root chakra and your throat chakra more than symbolic. Just as we plugged our root chakra into our foot chakra, improving the energy flow between those two areas, we want to plug our throat chakra into our root chakra. I personally envision a wire connecting my two chakras, but I've seen some people "hook" the two together, while others tie them together. Whatever method you use, picture connecting the two pools of energy. Picture them flowing into each other, the energies changing color as they pass between your root and throat chakras. This will help you walk your true path, because your chakras will support each other. Your throat chakra will teach your root chakra how to be more honest, improving both in the long run.

Chakra Six – Intuitive Chakra

Color:	**Indigo**
Element:	**Light**
Metal:	**Silver**

Your intuitive chakra is located in the middle of your forehead, right in that traditional third eye region, and it's responsible for insight. If your intuitive chakra is closed off, you will feel a lot of tension in your brow area. It will feel like there's a lot of weight there, because the energy is pooling up. It's not flowing correctly.

Learning to listen to and trust the intuitive chakra is difficult. It requires retraining the brain into new patterns of behavior, and your brain's not going to like it. To use our intuitive chakra, then, we have to shut down our brain. Quiet that rational, doubting side of your brain and learn to listen. Silence that primitive, survival-oriented part of the brain by redirecting blood elsewhere. Press on your neurovascular points to draw blood into the higher regions of the brain. If I'm alone

Take The FREE 3-Minute Chakra Healing Test. Find out how each of your 7 Chakras may be influencing your health and life

www.VelocityHousePresents.com/chakrahealing   **79**

and can get away with it, I often like to press my forehead flat on the ground. Once you've done that, just sit and think about whatever problems you face. Listen when the answer comes to you.

Another method you can use to quiet your mind requires a standard deck of cards. Talk aloud about your problems while flipping over the cards one at a time. Flipping the cards gives your mind something to focus on so it doesn't interfere with my intuitive chakra. This is the same principle behind thinking about your problems in the shower— your brain is just distracted enough to get out of the way of your intuitive chakra, allowing you to recognize insights you might miss otherwise. Other similar places to think about your problems include long drives on an empty highway, mowing the lawn and taking a long walk.

It's very helpful to ask the right questions, to touch your intuitive chakra. Rephrase the question so your intuition can answer. Narrow down your options and then go through them one by one and ask yourself if each is the right answer. Ask, "Is this correct?" and wait for an answer from your intuitive chakra.

Your intuitive chakra shows you the correct path. Your third eye is lighting your way. It's showing you the path. Picture your third eye like a big spotlight coming out of your forehead or like one of those headlamps that miners use. When you're out for a walk, imagine that indigo light shining out of your forehead and onto the ground in front of you. It's illuminating your path. It tells you that you're going in the right direction. It knows the way, even if you don't. When you do this, you both open your intuitive chakra further and learn to trust its insight.

Dream journals are also helpful. When you wake up in the middle of the night and feel like some insight is right on the edge of your brain, grab that journal and a pen and start writing down whatever you can remember. The more you chronicle your dreams, the better you'll get at recalling them. Your brain *wants* you to recall the insight you discovered in your dreams; that's why it woke you up in the first place. Learn to remember those insights in order to take advantage of them.

You can also do more intense meditations to get in contact with your intuitive chakra. Whenever you have a quiet moment, focus on your intuitive chakra. It's calming; it's simple once you get the hang of

Take The FREE 3-Minute Chakra Healing Test. Find out how each of your 7 Chakras may be influencing your health and life

80   *www.VelocityHousePresents.com/chakrahealing*

it, and it keeps the conduit open so you can draw upon that energy whenever necessary.

As your intuitive chakra fills and opens, it's important to connect it with your other chakras. All three of your lower chakras require energy from your sixth chakra in order to reach higher vibration levels. There are numerous ways you can forge a connection. Which you choose is a matter of personal preference. I normally opt to use "wires" between my chakras. I run circuits for the energy transfers, as if my body contained power cables. I've seen people use numerous other methods, however. Some people elect to "hook" their chakras together with their hands. They'll make a hook from the index fingers on both hands, placing the hooks on each of the two chakras they want to join. Then they'll pull the two hooks together, as if dragging part of the chakras along, and couple the two together. Whatever you'd like to use is fine, as long as the result is a free and open energy flow between the two chakras in question. Join your intuitive chakra to each of the three lower chakras: the root, the sacral, and the navel.

Chakra Seven – Crown Chakra

Color: **Purple**
Element: **Thought**
Metal: **Gold**

The crown chakra sits at the top of your head, just like a crown would. It's not just a pool of energy residing somewhere in your body, like the other chakras. Think of it like a large window. A portal into your mind, might be a better description. The crown chakra is a doorway. Just like a window, a portal, a doorway, your crown chakra has two states: open and shut.

One of the first things I recommend you do after opening your crown chakra is plugging it into your foot chakra. Visualize the wire running out of your crown chakra and into the base of your foot chakra, the energy flowing unimpeded. It's very important that we connect the crown and foot chakras because they need to work together. The crown chakra helps keep the foot chakra on the right path, and the foot chakra helps us not get overwhelmed by the energy in the crown chakra. We love these higher frequency energies that get drawn in through the crown chakra, but they're exhausting. When we connect to our foot chakra, we draw that energy out into the world and help our body use the energy from the spiritual realm instead of becoming distracted by it.

The first three methods of opening your crown chakra use your body to enhance your connection: headstands, head rolls and fasting. Headstands and head rolls concentrate your energies around your crown chakra. When you do a headstand, you are pressing your crown chakra against the ground and uniting those two energy reserves. This can be a very welcome feeling, and an easy technique to practice. Head rolls draw energy into your head and exploit the physical motion, enhancing your connection to the crown chakra. Fasting is effective because when we deny our physical needs, we enhane our spirituality. We give up our need for food to attain a higher spiritual connection.

You can use meditation and prayer to open your crown chakra. When we meditate or pray, we create a lot of higher vibration energies. We really begin to align our body to take advantage of those higher energies, and we naturally draw them in through our crown chakra. For the best results, I recommend making time to meditate or pray daily. Don't let it become routine or rote, because you'll find you're tuning out instead of actually focusing, but make time to connect with your crown chakra each day.

Maybe you believe in God, and you're ready to open your crown chakra, but you've yet to experience oneness with the divinity. You have a very clear idea of "God" and "self," and never the two shall meet. What I want you to do is unbox God. Remove the walls that you've placed around God in your mind. Now you might say, "I did that, and now there's nothing there." That's true. There's nothing in the box, and you can't *see* God anymore. Before, you could look at that box and say "There's God." Now you can't see the spiritual realm, and it's scary. It feels like there's nothing there at all.

Relax. God is still there. In fact, God is everywhere. You are a part of God, as is everything. When you box God up, you reduce the power of the spiritual realm. You're saying that God is only allowed in certain

Take The FREE 3-Minute Chakra Healing Test. Find out how each of your 7 Chakras may be influencing your health and life

82   www.VelocityHousePresents.com/chakrahealing

parts of your life. Let God go, and then trust that you're not alone. You're still being watched over. Let God out of the cell you've built.

You can improve our connection to your crown chakra with affirmations. This can help cement your connection with divinity and improve your sense of oneness. Place a hand on your crown chakra (the top of your head), focus on that purple window into your spirit, and begin affirming your link with the higher realm.

"*I am connected with the spiritual realm. I am receiving inspiration. I am receiving guidance. I deserve to know truth. I am true to myself. I am experiencing God. I hold God within me, as a part of me. I am connected with a higher purpose. I am not lost anymore. I know what to do. I know where to go. I am ready to face all obstacles in my path, with God beside me.*"

As always, feel free to replace "God" with any higher being you prefer. As you recite these affirmations, you should feel your sense of oneness, of connection, growing more powerful. I like to begin each day with this exercise. It keeps my crown chakra open and prepares my body to receive those higher frequency energies.

Connect your crown chakra with your navel chakra. Visualize wires or hooks connecting the two energy sources. This way, you connect your spiritual nature to your unique and grounded personality. The soul is helping guide the self along its path.

Take The FREE 3-Minute Chakra Healing Test. Find out how each of your 7 Chakras may be influencing your health and life

www.VelocityHousePresents.com/chakrahealing　　　**83**

Conclusion

If you've read this book from cover to cover, you now understand what goes into activating all of your chakras and keeping them balanced. Hopefully you feel healthier, better-adjusted and more productive even after this first read-through, but don't worry if you only see minute changes so far. Working with your chakras is a process that requires your continued investment. It may take time for the new philosophy to take hold in your life. I promise, though, that it's worth it. I'm still amazed, looking back at that lost twenty-something version of myself, a version that could have seen such a difference from simply connecting to my chakras. I'm so different now than I was back then, and I owe it all to working with my energy and connecting to my chakras.

In spite of your accomplishments so far, there's still quite a bit of work you can do. You know the basics now, and you're definitely discovering a new you, but you still need to use the tools. As I said at the beginning of this book, I recommend you work with your various energies at least a few times a week, especially as you get more comfortable with the process. Just like exercise, you'll build up endurance as time goes on. You'll be able to do more work each week.

Your energy is hopefully much better now than it was at the beginning of the book, but that doesn't mean you're done. Energy is constantly evolving, constantly in need of care. You can't neglect your chakras now that you've opened them. Spend a bit of time each day working on your energy. It doesn't have to be that long. Just half an hour daily will work (though I'd say sixty to ninety minutes is the sweet spot). I've even given you some low-effort exercises in this book so you can work on your energy without making a huge commitment.

Revisit any parts of the book that you felt particularly resonated with you. If you found a particular exercise or chapter that really spoke to you, that's great! It will help you open up those chakras and gain a better understanding of the way your body works. I encourage you to reread this book every once in a while and see if you connect with different parts each time.

The chakras contain a lot of depth, and a full understanding can take a lifetime. For now, it's great that you've started down this path. It will serve you well. As time goes on, new insights will come. Your new you won't be new forever. In fact, I find that I change much more rapidly when I'm open to my chakras than I did when I was closed off and withdrawn. The energies are evolving, and we must evolve with them. You're constantly in flux, constantly developing.

I hope you stay open to that process.

Let's take a moment for one more visualization. This is sort of a victory celebration of a visualization, because we're not really going to do anything with it. Let me show you how far you've come.

Picture all of your chakras at once. Start with your crown. Picture that purple spiritual portal at the top of your head. Then, picture the high-vibration energy being sucked in through that portal, moving down to your third eye area where it pools in an indigo reservoir. Then it trickles down to your throat, turning blue along the way. As it exits your throat, it changes to the green of your heart chakra, gathering in the center of your chest. It then turns yellow, as it makes its way down to your solar plexus and your navel chakra. Next it rests in your lower abdomen, orange like the fires of your sacral chakra. It descends to your groin, a red lake the energy field for your root chakra. Finally, it exits from your body through your feet, returning to the Earth.

It's a beautiful sight. It's a new you. And you accomplished it all by yourself!

Take The FREE 3-Minute Chakra Healing Test. Find out how each of your 7 Chakras may be influencing your health and life

86   *www.VelocityHousePresents.com/chakrahealing*

References

i   Leadbeater, C.W. *The Chakras*. Illinois: Theosophical Publishing House, 1927 (reprinted 2001).

ii   DeLiso, Tom. "The Foot Chakra." Accessed December, 2012. http://www.wisdomsdoor.com/hb/hhb-13.shtml

iii Atkinson, William Walker. *Thought Vibration Or the Law of Attraction in the Thought World*. Chicago: New Thought Publishing, 1906.

iv For more information, try Look, Carol. *Attracting Abundance with EFT*. Createspace Independent Publishing, 2005.

v   *It's a Wonderful Life*. Directed by Frank Capra. 1946.

vi Ponder, Catherine. *Open Your Mind to Prosperity*. California: Devorss and Company, 1984.

vii For more, see Sharamon, Shalila. *The Chakra Handbook*. Wisconsin: Lotus Press, 1991. Also consult a chart of chakra associations, such as the one provided by Project Inner Peace at *http://projectinnerpeace.org/wp-content/uploads/2011/10/Chakra-Chart2.jpg* or the one in Liz Simpson's *The Book of Chakra Healing*.

viii Gallegos, Eligio. "Animal Energy, The Chakra System, and Psychotherapy." *Journal of Transpersonal Psychology* 15 (1983): 125-136.

ix Bittlinger, Arnold. Archetypal Chakra: Meditations and Exercises of Opening Your Chakras. Weiser Books, 2001

x   Simpson, Liz. *The Book of Chakra Healing*. New York: Sterling Publishing Co., 1999.

xi Hanfileti, Dr. Peter. "Birth Energy Medicine and Your Baby." *Principles for Parents*. Accessed December, 2012. http://www.principlesforparents.com/birth-energy-medicine.html.

xii Virtue, Doreen. *Chakra Clearing*. Hay House. 2004.

xiii Simpson, Liz. *The Book of Chakra Healing*. New York: Sterling Publishing Co., 1999.

xiv Bittlinger, Arnold. Archetypal Chakra: Meditations and Exercises of Opening Your Chakras. Weiser Books, 2001.

xv For more on tantric sex, see: Lacroix, Nitya. *The Art of Tantric Sex*. DK Publishing, 1997 and White, D.G. *Tantra in Practice*. New Jersey: Princeton University Press, 2000.

xvi Nakano, Tamami, Makoto Kato, Yusuke Morito, Seishi Itoi, and Shigeru Kitazawa. "Blink-Related Momentary Activation of the Default Mode Network while Viewing Videos." *PNAS* 110 (2013): 702-706.

xvii Bugental, Daphne Blunt and Jeffrey Clayton Lewis. "The Paradoxical Misuse of Power by Those Who See Themselves as Powerless: How Does it Happen?" *Journal of Social Issues* 55 (1999): 51-64.

xviii   Sharamon, Shalila. *The Chakra Handbook*. Wisconsin: Lotus Press, 1991.

xix   Virtue, Doreen. *Chakra Clearing*. Hay House. 2004. Also, see *www.treeoflifeawakening.com/* for further information.

xx   Craig, Gary. *The EFT Manual, Sixth Ed*. Independently published, 2011. Retrieved December, 2012. http://www.spiritual-web.com/downloads/eftmanual.pdf.

xxi   Johari, Harish. *Chakras: Energy centers of transformation*. Inner Traditions/Bear & Co, 2000.

xxii   Simpson, Liz. *The Book of Chakra Healing*. New York: Sterling Publishing Co., 1999.

xxiii   Lennon, John and Paul McCartney. "The End," *Abbey Road*. Apple. 1969.

xxiv   *The King's Speech*. Directed by Tom Hooper. 2010.

xxv   Sharamon, Shalila. *The Chakra Handbook*. Wisconsin: Lotus Press, 1991.

xxvi   Ross Cohen, L. P. C., and I. CADC. "Using the Chakra System in Psychotherapy." 2006.

xxvii   Leadbeater, C.W. *The Chakras*. Illinois: Theosophical Publishing House, 1927 (reprinted 2001).

xxviii Virtue, Doreen. *Chakra Clearing*. Hay House. 2004.

xxix   Simpson, Liz. *The Book of Chakra Healing*. New York: Sterling Publishing Co., 1999.

xxx   Greenwood, Michael. "Acupuncture and the chakras." *Medical Acupuncture* 17, no. 3 (2006): 27-32.

xxxi   See Boyer, Janet. "Chakra 7 – The Crown Chakra." Accessed December, 2012. http://www.janetboyer.com/Chakra_7-The_Crown_Chakra.html.

xxxii   Simpson, Liz. *The Book of Chakra Healing*. New York: Sterling Publishing Co., 1999.

Take The FREE 3-Minute Chakra Healing Test. Find out how each of your 7 Chakras may be influencing your health and life

88   *www.VelocityHousePresents.com/chakrahealing*

CPSIA information can be obtained at www.ICGtesting.com
Printed in the USA
LVOW06s0124151113

361408LV00009B/230/P